Better Homes and Gardens®

stir-fries

COOKING FOR TODAY

BETTER HOMES AND GARDENS® BOOKS
Des Moines

BETTER HOMES AND GARDENS® BOOKS
An Imprint of Meredith® Books
President, Book Group: Joseph J. Ward
Vice President and Editorial Director: Elizabeth P. Rice
Executive Editor: Nancy N. Green
Managing Editor: Christopher Cavanaugh
Art Director: Ernest Shelton
Test Kitchen Director: Sharon Stilwell

STIR-FRIES
Editor: Mary Major Williams
Writer: Joanne G. Fullan
Associate Art Director: Tom Wegner
Graphic Production Coordinator: Paula Forest
Production Manager: Doug Johnston
Test Kitchen Product Supervisor: Marilyn Cornelius
Food Stylists: Lynn Blanchard, Janet Pittman, Jennifer Peterson
Photographers: Mike Dieter, Scott Little
Cover Photographer: Andy Lyons

On the cover: Turkey-Apricot Stir-Fry (see recipe, page 65)

Meredith Corporation Corporate Officers:
Chairman of the Executive Committee: E. T. Meredith III
Chairman of the Board, President and Chief Executive Officer: Jack D. Rehm
Group Presidents: Joseph J. Ward, Books; William T. Kerr, Magazines; Philip A. Jones, Broadcasting;
    Allen L. Sabbag, Real Estate
Vice Presidents: Leo R. Armatis, Corporate Relations; Thomas G. Fisher, General Counsel and Secretary;
    Larry D. Hartsook, Finance; Michael A. Sell, Treasurer; Kathleen J. Zehr, Controller and Assistant Secretary

WE CARE!

All of us at Better Homes and Gardens® Books are dedicated to providing you with the information
and ideas you need to create tasty foods. We welcome your comments and suggestions. Write us at:
Better Homes and Gardens® Books, Cookbook Editorial Department, 1716 Locust St., Des Moines,
IA 50309-3023

Our seal assures you that every recipe in *Stir-Fries* has been
tested in the Better Homes and Gardens® Test Kitchen.
This means that each recipe is practical and reliable, and
meets our high standards of taste appeal. We guarantee
your satisfaction with this book for as long as you own it.

First Edition. Printing Number and Year: 15 14 13 21 11   02 01 00 99
Library of Congress Catalog Card Number: 94-75962
ISBN: 0-696-02568-X

One of the fastest, most fuel-efficient ways to cook is an ancient method known as stir-frying. It originated out of necessity in the sparsely forested areas of southern China where charcoal for cooking was scarce. Because of its thrifty use of both time and fuel, this cooking technique spread throughout Asia and the rest of the world. Here in the West, where we value convenience and efficiency, stir-frying continues to grow in popularity as a quick and easy means to provide good-tasting, healthful meals. So whether you're looking for meat, poultry, seafood, or meatless main dishes, or a side dish to complete your menu, you'll find them here.

Choose from classic Chinese specialties such as Kung Pao Chicken, Shrimp Lo Mein, and Beef and Vegetables in Oyster Sauce. Or, sample stir-fries from other parts of Asia—Coconut Shrimp with Garlic from Thailand, Asian Vinegar Chicken from Vietnam, and Fragrant Spiced Chicken from Malaysia. And just because it's stir-fried doesn't mean it has to be Oriental. We've adapted Italian, Tex-Mex, Greek, and everyday American recipes to this quick-cooking method with great-tasting results.

CONTENTS

STIR-FRYING BASICS..4

MEAT 6

POULTRY 40

FISH AND SEAFOOD 76

MEATLESS MAIN DISHES....................................108

SIDE DISHES..122

INDEX..142

WHAT ABOUT THE WOK?

■ Woks come in two basic shapes. The classic round-bottom wok with its accompanying ring stand is appropriate for use on a gas range. It is not, however, recommended for the electric range. The flat-bottom wok can be used on either an electric or gas range. No ring stand is needed to support this type of wok because the flat bottom allows the pan to rest directly on the burner. Electric woks are also available. They have the great advantage of being portable, so they are well suited to table-top cooking. However, most electric woks don't maintain the high temperatures ideally needed for stir-frying, so the food may take a little longer to cook.

■ Woks made of aluminum and stainless steel require minimal maintenance. Simply wash in hot soapy water after each use. Some aluminum and stainless steel woks have nonstick interior coatings that need seasoning. (Follow the manufacturer's directions for seasoning.)

■ Steel woks are still the most popular, although they require more care. They come from the factory protected with a rust-resistant coating which must be removed before use. To remove the coating, scrub the wok, inside and out, with a plastic scouring pad and hot soapy water. Dry thoroughly, first with a towel and then by heating it on your range for several minutes. When thoroughly dry, season the new wok by evenly coating the inside surface with 2 tablespoons of cooking oil. Heat over high heat till both the wok and the oil are very hot. Allow to cool, and then rub in the oil with a paper towel. After each use, the wok should be soaked in hot water (detergent is not recommended) and scrubbed with a plastic scouring pad. Rinse and dry the wok. Then heat it on the range to dry completely. Add 1 teaspoon of cooking oil to the wok and rub it in with a paper towel.

■ All woks should be stored in a well-ventilated place. Long periods in a warm airless cupboard can cause the oil used on a seasoned wok to turn rancid.

A WORD ABOUT COOKING OIL

■ The total amount of cooking oil needed in a recipe will depend on the type of wok or skillet used. Those with a nonstick lining tend to use less oil than their counterparts.

■ As a matter of safety, begin heating the cooking oil in a cold wok. Avoid heating the wok first before adding the oil. If more oil is needed during the stir-fry process, push the meat and/or vegetables to the side of the wok and pour a small amount of oil directly into the center; allow it to heat up before continuing to stir-fry.

GETTING READY

■ The single most important thing you need to do before you even think about heating your wok is prepare. Since stir-frying is a very rapid cooking technique, it requires the constant involvement of the cook. Once you begin, there is no time between steps to stop and prepare ingredients, so it's essential that everything be organized beforehand.

■ Cut and measure all ingredients. Meats and vegetables should be uniformly sliced to ensure fast, even cooking. If you partially freeze the meat, you'll be able to cut thin slices without difficulty.

■ Marinate, precook, or preseason any of the ingredients as directed in the recipe.

■ Combine all the ingredients for the sauce.

■ Cook the rice, pasta, or noodles called for in the recipe.

STEPS FOR STIR-FRYING

1. Begin by heating the oil in a wok or large skillet. When the oil is hot, add garlic, gingerroot, and/or onion, and stir-fry for just 15 seconds. This will release the flavors of the seasonings into the oil and subsequently season the vegetables, meat, and sauce.

2. Next add the vegetables according to the amount of time each needs to cook. The denser and tougher ones, like carrots, go into the wok first. The more tender ones, including pea pods and bean sprouts, are added last. Use a wooden spoon or a long-handled Chinese spatula for stir-frying. A Chinese spatula resembles a shovel and is ideally suited for the constant lifting and turning of ingredients that ensures even cooking. When done, remove the vegetables from the wok.

3. Meat, poultry, fish, or seafood are stir-fried next. To ensure that the meat cooks quickly and the juices are sealed in, do not overload the wok. Cook no more than 12 ounces of meat at a time. If larger amounts are called for, stir-fry the meat in two or more smaller batches and then return all of the meat to the wok.

4. The sauce mixture is now ready to add. Push the meat to the side of the wok, stir the sauce mixture, and pour it directly into the center of the wok or skillet. Cook and stir the sauce till it is thickened and bubbly. Now return the vegetables to the wok. Gently toss together all of the ingredients to coat with the sauce. Allow the mixture to heat through and serve immediately.

BEEF AND VEGETABLES IN OYSTER SAUCE

Oyster sauce, a favorite seasoning in Cantonese dishes, is thick and brown and, as the name implies, made from an extract of oysters. It is available in both bottles and cans and should be refrigerated after opening.

1 pound beef top round steak
¼ cup oyster sauce
1 tablespoon soy sauce
⅛ teaspoon pepper
1 tablespoon cooking oil
3 cloves garlic, minced
1 medium onion, cut into thin wedges
4 cups bok choy, cut into 1-inch pieces
2 cups fresh pea pods, strings removed, or one 6-ounce package frozen pea pods, thawed
2 small tomatoes, cut into thin wedges (1½ cups)
2 cups hot cooked rice

Trim fat from beef. Partially freeze beef. Thinly slice across grain into bite-size strips. Set aside.

For sauce, in a small bowl stir together oyster sauce, soy sauce, and pepper. Set aside.

Pour cooking oil into a wok or large skillet. (Add more oil as necessary during cooking.) Preheat over medium-high heat. Stir-fry garlic in hot oil for 15 seconds. Add onion; stir-fry for 2 minutes. Add bok choy and pea pods; stir-fry about 3 minutes or till vegetables are crisp-tender. Remove vegetables from the wok.

Add *half* of the beef to the hot wok. Stir-fry for 2 to 3 minutes or to desired doneness. Remove beef from the wok. Repeat with remaining beef. Return all of the beef to the wok. Push the beef from the center of the wok.

Stir the sauce. Add sauce to the center of the wok. Cook and stir till bubbly. Return cooked vegetables to the wok. Add tomatoes. Stir all ingredients together to coat with sauce. Cook and stir for 1 to 2 minutes or till heated through. Serve immediately over hot cooked rice. Makes 4 servings.

Nutrition information per serving: 382 calories, 34 g protein, 39 g carbohydrate, 10 g fat (3 g saturated fat), 77 mg cholesterol, 883 mg sodium, 944 mg potassium.

SWEET-AND-SOUR STEAK

The sweet-and-sour dishes of Canton are among the most familiar types of Chinese food. They are said to have evolved in response to the demanding tastes of the foreigners in this large port city.

8 ounces beef top round steak
1 small orange
1 15¼-ounce can pineapple chunks
   (juice pack)
2 tablespoons vinegar
2 tablespoons soy sauce
1 tablespoon cornstarch
1 tablespoon brown sugar
⅛ teaspoon ground red pepper
1 tablespoon cooking oil
1 medium green sweet pepper, cut into
   1-inch pieces (1 cup)
1 small onion, cut into thin wedges
2 cups hot cooked rice
   Orange slices (optional)

Trim fat from beef. Partially freeze beef. Thinly slice across grain into bite-size strips. Set aside.

Peel and section orange. Cut sections in half lengthwise. Set aside.

For sauce, drain pineapple reserving juice. Pour *½ cup* of the reserved juice into a small bowl. (Reserve remaining juice for another use.) Stir in vinegar, soy sauce, cornstarch, brown sugar, and ground red pepper. Set aside.

Pour cooking oil into a wok or large skillet. (Add more oil as necessary during cooking.) Preheat over medium-high heat. Stir-fry green pepper and onion in hot oil for 3 to 4 minutes or till crisp-tender. Remove vegetables from the wok.

Add beef to the hot wok. Stir-fry for 2 to 3 minutes or to desired doneness. Push beef from the center of the wok.

Stir sauce. Add sauce to the center of the wok. Cook and stir till thickened and bubbly. Return cooked vegetables to the wok. Add pineapple chunks. Stir all ingredients together to coat with sauce. Cook and stir for 2 minutes more or till heated through. Stir in orange slices. Serve immediately over hot cooked rice. Garnish with additional orange sections, if desired. Makes 4 servings.

Nutrition information per serving: 326 calories, 17 g protein, 51 g carbohydrate, 7 g fat (2 g saturated fat), 36 mg cholesterol, 545 mg sodium, 521 mg potassium.

THAI BEEF LARNAR

In Thai cuisine, fish sauce is a common ingredient used to salt foods. In this recipe it seasons the Nam Prik—Thailand's version of bottled hot pepper sauce.

     Nam Prik (see recipe below)
1   **pound beef top round steak**
1   **tablespoon cooking oil**
4   **cups broccoli flowerets**
2   **cups hot cooked rice**
     Chili flower (optional)

Prepare Nam Prik. Set aside. Trim fat from beef. Partially freeze beef. Thinly slice across grain into bite-size strips. Set aside.

Pour cooking oil into a wok or large skillet. (Add more oil as necessary during cooking.) Preheat over medium-high heat. Stir-fry broccoli in hot oil for 3 to 4 minutes or till crisp-tender. Remove broccoli from the wok.

Add *half* of the beef to the hot wok. Stir-fry for 2 to 3 minutes or to desired doneness. Remove beef from the wok. Repeat with remaining beef. Return all beef to the wok.

Stir Nam Prik. Add Nam Prik to the center of the wok. Return broccoli to the wok. Stir all ingredients together to coat with Nam Prik. Bring to boiling. Cover and cook 1 minute more or till heated through. Serve immediately with hot cooked rice. Garnish with chili flower, if desired. Makes 4 servings.

Nam Prik: Wearing rubber gloves, cut open 2 to 4 *dried red chili peppers.* Discard stems and seeds; cut up peppers. Place peppers in bowl and cover with *boiling water.* Let peppers stand for 45 minutes to 1 hour. Drain. (*Or,* substitute ½ to 1 teaspoon *crushed red pepper* and continue as directed.) In a blender container combine peppers or crushed red pepper; ¼ cup *water;* 2 tablespoons *lemon juice;* 2 tablespoons *soy sauce;* 1 tablespoon *cooking oil;* 1 to 1½ teaspoons *fish sauce or nuoc cham;* and 2 to 4 cloves *garlic,* quartered. Cover and blend till mixture is nearly smooth.

Nutrition information per serving: 363 calories, 33 g protein, 30 g carbohydrate, 13 g fat (3 g saturated fat), 73 mg cholesterol, 662 mg sodium, 742 mg potassium.

SOUTHWESTERN STIR-FRY

Just because it comes out of a wok doesn't mean it has to taste Chinese! The proof is in the eating, so why not sample this Mexican-style stir-fry?

1   cup salsa
2   teaspoons cornstarch
8   8-inch flour tortillas
1   tablespoon cooking oil
1   medium green sweet pepper, cut into
       strips
1   12-ounce can whole kernel corn,
       drained
3   green onions, bias-sliced into 1-inch
       pieces (½ cup)
1   pound lean ground beef
10   cherry tomatoes, halved
½   cup shredded cheddar cheese or
       Monterey Jack cheese with jalapeño
       peppers (2 ounces)
       Cilantro sprigs (optional)

For sauce, in a small bowl stir together salsa and cornstarch. Set aside.

Stack tortillas; wrap in foil. Heat in a 350° oven about 10 minutes or till warm. *Or,* place tortillas, *half* at a time, between layers of microwave-safe paper towels; micro-cook on 100% power (high) for 1½ to 2 minutes or till warm.

Pour cooking oil into a wok or large skillet. (Add more oil as necessary during cooking.) Preheat over medium-high heat. Stir-fry sweet pepper, corn, and green onions for 2 minutes or till sweet pepper is crisp-tender. Remove vegetables from the wok.

Crumble beef into the hot wok. Stir-fry for 2 to 3 minutes or till brown, stirring only as necessary. Drain off fat. Push meat from the center of the wok.

Stir sauce. Add sauce to center of the wok. Cook and stir till thickened and bubbly. Return cooked vegetables to the wok. Stir all ingredients together to coat with sauce. Stir in tomatoes; reduce heat. Cover and cook for 1 minute more or till heated through. Serve immediately with tortillas. Sprinkle with cheese. Garnish with cilantro, if desired. Makes 4 servings.

Nutrition information per serving: 634 calories, 31 g protein, 64 g carbohydrate, 29 g fat (10 g saturated fat), 85 mg cholesterol, 1,042 mg sodium, 828 mg potassium.

Szechwan Shredded Beef and Carrots

China's Szechwan province has a distinctively hot and spicy cuisine. The spicy heat in this dish is tempered by the spicy sweetness of hoisin sauce.

12 ounces beef top round steak
2   tablespoons dry sherry
2   tablespoons soy sauce
1   tablespoon hoisin sauce
1   tablespoon hot bean sauce or hot bean paste
2   teaspoons sugar
2   teaspoons grated gingerroot
1   teaspoon toasted sesame oil
½   teaspoon crushed red pepper
¼   teaspoon black pepper
1   clove garlic, minced
1   tablespoon cooking oil
3   medium carrots, cut into julienne strips (1½ cups)
2   cups hot cooked rice
2   green onions, thinly bias-sliced (¼ cup)

Trim fat from beef. Partially freeze beef. Thinly slice across grain into bite-size strips. Cut strips in half lengthwise. Set aside.

For sauce, in a small bowl stir together sherry, soy sauce, hoisin sauce, bean sauce or paste, sugar, gingerroot, sesame oil, crushed red pepper, black pepper, and garlic. Set aside.

Pour cooking oil into a wok or large skillet. (Add more oil as necessary during cooking.) Preheat over medium-high heat. Stir-fry carrots in hot oil for 3 to 4 minutes or till crisp-tender. Remove carrots from the wok.

Add beef to the hot wok. Stir-fry for 2 to 3 minutes or to desired doneness. Push beef from the center of the wok.

Stir sauce. Add sauce to the center of the wok. Cook and stir till bubbly. Return cooked carrots to the wok. Stir all ingredients together to coat with sauce. Cook and stir for 2 minutes more or till heated through. Serve immediately with hot cooked rice. Sprinkle rice with green onions. Makes 4 servings.

Nutrition information per serving: 314 calories, 24 g protein, 31 g carbohydrate, 9 g fat (2 g saturated fat), 54 mg cholesterol, 1,086 mg sodium, 501 mg potassium.

Greek-Style Beef with Vegetables

Cinnamon, cloves, brown sugar, vinegar, and tomato paste give this fast-fix wok dish the distinctive flavor of Stefado (Greek beef stew).

12 ounces beef top round steak or lean
      boneless lamb
3   medium potatoes, cut into ¾-inch
      cubes (3 cups)
2   medium carrots, roll-cut (1 cup)
1   cup water
1   tablespoon cornstarch
1   tablespoon brown sugar
¾   teaspoon salt
½   teaspoon ground cinnamon
¼   teaspoon pepper
⅛   teaspoon ground cloves
½   of a 6-ounce can tomato paste (⅓ cup)
½   cup pitted ripe olives
1   tablespoon cooking oil
2   cloves garlic, minced
2   medium onions, cut into thin wedges
1   medium green, red, or yellow sweet
      pepper, cut into strips
2   tablespoons red wine vinegar

Trim fat from beef or lamb. Partially freeze meat. Thinly slice across grain into bite-size strips. Set aside.

In a medium saucepan precook potatoes and carrots, covered, in enough boiling water to cover about 10 minutes or till just tender. Drain. Set aside.

For sauce, in a small bowl stir together water, cornstarch, brown sugar, salt, cinnamon, pepper, and ground cloves. Stir in tomato paste. Add olives. Set aside.

Pour cooking oil into a wok or large skillet. (Add more oil as necessary during cooking.) Preheat over medium-high heat. Stir-fry garlic in hot oil for 15 seconds. Add onions; stir-fry for 1 minute. Add sweet pepper; stir-fry about 2 minutes or till crisp-tender. Remove pepper mixture from the wok.

Add meat to the hot wok. Stir-fry for 2 to 3 minutes or to desired doneness. Push meat from the center of the wok.

Stir sauce. Add sauce to the center of the wok. Cook and stir till thickened and bubbly. Stir in vinegar. Return pepper mixture to the wok. Add precooked potatoes and carrots. Stir all ingredients together to coat with sauce. Cover and cook for 1 to 2 minutes more or till heated through. Serve immediately. Makes 4 servings.

Nutrition information per serving: 376 calories, 26 g protein, 48 g carbohydrate, 11 g fat (2 g saturated fat), 54 mg cholesterol, 568 mg sodium, 1,279 mg potassium.

SPICY THAI GINGER BEEF

Thai cooking is strongly influenced by both Chinese and Indian cuisines. In fact, the Thai people migrated from China's Yunnan province in the 13th century.

12 ounces beef top round steak
 1 tablespoon fish sauce
 1 tablespoon water
 1 teaspoon finely shredded lime peel
 1 tablespoon lime juice
 1 teaspoon sugar
 1 tablespoon cooking oil
 2 medium zucchini, cut into julienne
       strips (2 cups)
 6 green onions, bias-cut into 1-inch
       pieces (1 cup)
 1 fresh, pickled, or canned jalapeño
       pepper, seeded and finely chopped
 2 teaspoons grated gingerroot
 3 cloves garlic, minced
 2 cups hot cooked rice sticks or rice
 2 tablespoons snipped cilantro

Trim fat from beef. Partially freeze beef. Thinly slice across grain into bite-size strips. Set aside.

For sauce, in a small bowl stir together fish sauce, water, lime peel, lime juice, and sugar. Set aside.

Pour cooking oil into a wok or large skillet. (Add more oil as necessary during cooking.) Preheat over medium-high heat. Stir-fry zucchini in hot oil for 1 to 2 minutes or till crisp-tender. Remove zucchini from the wok. Add green onions to the hot wok; stir-fry for 1½ minutes. Remove green onions from the wok.

Add jalapeño pepper, gingerroot, and garlic to the hot wok. Stir-fry for 15 seconds. Add beef; stir-fry for 2 to 3 minutes or to desired doneness. Return zucchini and green onions to the wok.

Add sauce. Cook and stir for 2 minutes more or till heated through. Serve immediately with hot cooked rice sticks or rice. Sprinkle with cilantro. Makes 3 servings.

Nutrition information per serving: 339 calories, 31 g protein, 30 g carbohydrate, 10 g fat (3 g saturated fat), 74 mg cholesterol, 242 mg sodium, 689 mg potassium.

ORANGE-BEEF STIR-FRY

In this mild version of a classic Szechwan recipe, we've rounded out the dish with the addition of crisp water chestnuts and fresh spinach.

12 ounces beef top round steak
1   teaspoon finely shredded orange peel
½   cup orange juice
1   tablespoon cornstarch
1   tablespoon soy sauce
1   teaspoon sugar
1   teaspoon instant beef bouillon
      granules
1   tablespoon cooking oil
4   green onions, bias-sliced into 1-inch
      pieces (⅔ cup)
1   clove garlic, minced
6   cups coarsely shredded fresh spinach
      (8 ounces)
½   of an 8-ounce can sliced water
      chestnuts, drained
2   cups hot cooked rice
     Slivered orange peel (optional)

Trim fat from beef. Partially freeze beef. Thinly slice across grain into bite-size strips. Set aside.

For sauce, in a small bowl stir together orange peel, orange juice, cornstarch, soy sauce, sugar, and bouillon granules. Set aside.

Pour cooking oil into a wok or large skillet. (Add more oil as necessary during cooking.) Preheat over medium-high heat. Stir-fry green onions and garlic in hot oil for 1 minute. Remove green onion mixture from the wok.

Add beef to the hot wok. Stir-fry for 2 to 3 minutes or to desired doneness. Push beef from the center of the wok.

Stir sauce. Add sauce to the center of the wok. Cook and stir till thickened and bubbly. Return green onion mixture to the wok. Add spinach and water chestnuts. Stir all ingredients together to coat with sauce. Cover and cook for 1 minute more or till heated through. Serve immediately over hot cooked rice. Sprinkle with slivered orange peel, if desired. Makes 4 servings.

Nutrition information per serving: 315 calories, 26 g protein, 35 g carbohydrate, 8 g fat (2 g saturated fat), 54 mg cholesterol, 582 mg sodium, 891 mg potassium.

SZECHWAN BEEF STIR-FRY

The heat in this dish comes from three sources: hot bean sauce, Szechwan peppercorns, and chili oil.

12 ounces boneless beef sirloin steak
 6 dried mushrooms (1 cup), such as
      shiitake or wood ear mushrooms
 ¼ cup hot bean sauce or hot bean paste
 ¼ cup dry sherry
 2 tablespoons soy sauce
 ¾ teaspoon whole Szechwan pepper or
      whole black pepper, crushed
 ½ teaspoon cornstarch
 ½ to 1 teaspoon chili oil
 1 tablespoon cooking oil
 2 medium carrots, bias-sliced (1 cup)
 1 clove garlic, minced
 1½ cups broccoli flowerets or one
      10-ounce package frozen cut
      broccoli, thawed
 1 8-ounce can bamboo shoots, drained
 2 cups hot cooked rice
 2 green onions, cut into slivers (¼ cup)

Trim fat from beef. Partially freeze beef. Thinly slice across grain into bite-size strips. Set aside.

In a small bowl cover mushrooms with warm water. Let soak for 30 minutes. Rinse and squeeze mushrooms to drain thoroughly. Discard stems. Thinly slice mushrooms. Set aside.

For sauce, in a small bowl stir together bean sauce or paste, sherry, soy sauce, crushed Szechwan pepper or black pepper, cornstarch, and chili oil. Set aside.

Pour cooking oil into a wok or large skillet. (Add more oil as necessary during cooking.) Preheat over medium-high heat. Stir-fry carrots and garlic in hot oil for 2 minutes. Add broccoli; stir-fry for 2 minutes. Add bamboo shoots and mushrooms; stir-fry for 1 to 2 minutes more or till vegetables are crisp-tender. Remove vegetables from wok.

Add beef to the hot wok. Stir-fry for 2 to 3 minutes or to desired doneness. Push beef from the center of the wok.

Stir sauce. Add sauce to the center of the wok. Cook and stir till thickened and bubbly. Return cooked vegetables to the wok. Stir all ingredients together to coat with sauce. Cook and stir for 1 minute more or till heated through. Serve immediately with hot cooked rice. Garnish with slivered green onions. Makes 4 servings.

Nutrition information per serving: 387 calories, 25 g protein, 53 g carbohydrate, 9 g fat (2 g saturated fat), 49 mg cholesterol, 1,615 mg sodium, 961 mg potassium.

LAMB AND BEAN RAGOUT

This saucy lamb dish gets a protein boost from a vegetable source—white kidney beans.

8   ounces lean boneless lamb or beef top
       round steak
8   ounces whole fresh mushrooms,
       (3 cups)
1   tablespoon cooking oil
2   cloves garlic, minced
2   medium onions, cut into thin wedges
1   medium yellow summer squash,
       halved lengthwise and sliced
       (1¼ cups)
1   tablespoon snipped fresh basil or
       1 teaspoon dried basil, crushed
1   16-ounce can tomatoes, cut up
1   15- to 19-ounce can cannellini beans
       (white kidney beans), rinsed and
       drained
½   teaspoon salt
⅛   teaspoon pepper
8   ounces rigatoni or ziti, cooked and
       drained
    Fresh basil sprigs (optional)

Trim fat from lamb or beef. Partially freeze meat. Thinly slice across grain into bite-size strips. Set aside. Cut any large mushrooms in half. Set aside.

Pour cooking oil into a wok or large skillet. (Add more oil as necessary during cooking.) Preheat over medium-high heat. Stir-fry garlic in hot oil for 15 seconds. Add onions; stir-fry for 3 minutes. Add mushrooms, squash, and basil; stir-fry for 3 to 4 minutes or till vegetables are crisp-tender. Remove vegetables from the wok.

Add meat to the hot wok. Stir-fry for 2 to 3 minutes or to desired doneness. Return cooked vegetables to the wok.

Add *undrained* tomatoes, drained beans, salt, and pepper. Stir all ingredients together. Cook and stir for 3 to 4 minutes more or till slightly thickened. Serve immediately over hot cooked pasta. Garnish with basil, if desired. Makes 4 to 5 servings.

Nutrition information per serving: 439 calories, 26 g protein, 73 g carbohydrate, 8 g fat (2 g saturated fat), 29 mg cholesterol, 644 mg sodium, 975 mg potassium.

GREEK LAMB STIR-FRY

Oregano and rosemary join with fresh lemon juice, olive oil, and feta cheese to lend this delicious lamb dish some of the characteristic flavors of Greece.

8   ounces lean boneless lamb
1   tablespoon cooking oil
1   tablespoon lemon juice or balsamic
        vinegar
½   teaspoon dried rosemary, crushed
½   teaspoon dried oregano, crushed
¼   teaspoon pepper
1   tablespoon cooking oil
1   clove garlic, minced
1   medium carrot, thinly bias-sliced
        (½ cup)
1   small red onion, thinly sliced (⅓ cup)
4   cups torn fresh spinach
        (about 5 ounces)
2   small tomatoes, cut into thin wedges
2   cups hot cooked rice (optional)
¼   cup crumbled feta cheese (1 ounce)

Trim fat from lamb. Partially freeze lamb. Thinly slice across grain into bite-size strips. Set aside.

For sauce, in a small bowl combine 1 tablespoon oil, lemon juice or vinegar, rosemary, oregano, and pepper. Set aside.

Pour 1 tablespoon cooking oil into a wok or large skillet. (Add more oil as necessary during cooking.) Preheat over medium-high heat. Stir-fry garlic in hot oil for 15 seconds. Add carrot and onion; stir-fry for 3 to 4 minutes or till crisp-tender. Remove vegetables from wok.

Add lamb to the hot wok. Stir-fry for 2 to 3 minutes or to desired doneness. Return cooked carrot and onion to the wok. Add sauce, spinach, and tomato wedges. Stir all ingredients together to coat with sauce. Remove from heat. Serve immediately over hot cooked rice, if desired. Top with crumbled feta cheese. Makes 3 servings.

Nutrition information per serving: 243 calories, 16 g protein, 11 g carbohydrate, 16 g fat (4 g saturated fat), 45 mg cholesterol, 208 mg sodium, 820 mg potassium.

STIR-FRIED PORK AND JICAMA

Though jicama (HE-kuh-muh) is a Mexican vegetable, it adds some crispness to this Chinese-inspired dish.

1 pound lean boneless pork
½ cup cold water
¼ cup dry sherry
¼ cup soy sauce
4 teaspoons cornstarch
1 tablespoon cooking oil
1 teaspoon grated gingerroot
1 clove garlic, minced
½ of a medium jicama, peeled and cut
    into julienne strips (1 cup)
1 medium red and/or green sweet
    pepper, cut into thin strips
1 green onion, sliced (2 tablespoons)
2 cups shredded spinach or Chinese
    cabbage
2 cups hot cooked rice

Trim fat from pork. Partially freeze pork. Thinly slice across grain into bite-size strips. Set aside.

For sauce, in a small bowl stir together water, sherry, soy sauce, and cornstarch. Set aside.

Pour cooking oil into a wok or large skillet. (Add more oil as necessary during cooking.) Preheat over medium-high heat. Stir-fry gingerroot and garlic in hot oil for 15 seconds. Add jicama, sweet pepper strips, and green onion; stir-fry 1 to 2 minutes or till crisp-tender. Remove vegetables from the wok.

Add *half* of the pork to the hot wok. Stir-fry for 2 to 3 minutes or till no pink remains. Remove pork from the wok. Repeat with remaining pork. Return all of the pork to wok. Push pork from center of wok.

Stir sauce. Add sauce to the center of the wok. Cook and stir till thickened and bubbly. Add cooked vegetables. Stir all ingredients together to coat with sauce. Add spinach or cabbage. Cook and stir 1 to 2 minutes more or till heated through. Serve immediately with hot cooked rice. Makes 4 servings.

Nutrition information per serving: 341 calories, 21 g protein, 35 g carbohydrate, 11 g fat (3 g saturated fat), 51 mg cholesterol, 1,080 mg sodium, 396 mg potassium.

CASHEW PORK AND BROCCOLI

The Portuguese brought the cashew from the New World to India and East Africa in the fifteenth century. From there it traveled to China and worked its way into Chinese cuisine.

12   ounces lean boneless pork
 2   tablespoons soy sauce
 2   teaspoons toasted sesame oil
 2   teaspoons grated gingerroot
 2   cloves garlic, minced
 ½   cup hoisin sauce
 ½   cup water
 2   tablespoons soy sauce
 1   tablespoon cornstarch
 1   teaspoon sugar
 ⅛   teaspoon crushed red pepper
 1   tablespoon cooking oil
 2   medium onions, cut into thin wedges
 2   stalks celery, thinly bias-sliced (1 cup)
 3   cups broccoli flowerets
 2   cups hot cooked rice
 ½   cup dry roasted cashews

Trim fat from pork. Partially freeze pork. Thinly slice across grain into bite-size strips. In a medium bowl stir together pork, 2 tablespoons soy sauce, sesame oil, gingerroot, and garlic. Cover and refrigerate for 1 to 2 hours.

For sauce, in a small bowl stir together hoisin sauce, water, 2 tablespoons soy sauce, cornstarch, sugar, and crushed red pepper. Set sauce aside.

Pour cooking oil into a wok or large skillet. (Add more oil as necessary during cooking.) Preheat over medium-high heat. Stir-fry onions and celery in hot oil for 1 minute. Add broccoli; stir-fry for 3 to 4 minutes or till the vegetables are crisp-tender. Remove vegetables from the wok.

Add pork mixture to the hot wok. Stir-fry for 2 to 3 minutes or till no pink remains. Push pork from the center of the wok.

Stir sauce. Add sauce to the center of the wok. Cook and stir till sauce is thickened and bubbly. Return cooked vegetables to the wok. Stir all ingredients together to coat with sauce. Cover and cook for 1 minute more or till heated through. Serve immediately with hot cooked rice. Sprinkle with cashews. Makes 4 servings.

Nutrition information per serving: 480 calories, 21 g protein, 42 g carbohydrate, 26 g fat (5 g saturated fat), 38 mg cholesterol, 1,554 mg sodium, 579 mg potassium.

SZECHWAN PORK WITH PEPPERS

Green and red sweet peppers plus the spicy sweetness of hoisin sauce contrast nicely with the pleasant hotness of the dish. If you want to turn up the heat, add more hot bean sauce.

12 ounces lean boneless pork
3 tablespoons hoisin sauce
1 tablespoon hot bean sauce or hot bean paste
1 tablespoon soy sauce
1 teaspoon sugar
1 tablespoon cooking oil
1 teaspoon grated gingerroot
4 cloves garlic, thinly sliced
2 medium red sweet peppers, cut into 1-inch squares (2 cups)
2 medium green sweet peppers, cut into 1-inch squares (2 cups)
2 cups hot cooked noodles or rice

Trim fat from pork. Partially freeze pork. Thinly slice across grain into bite-size strips. Set aside.

For sauce, in a small bowl stir together hoisin sauce, bean sauce or paste, soy sauce, and sugar. Set aside.

Pour cooking oil into a wok or large skillet. (Add more oil as necessary during cooking.) Preheat over medium-high heat. Stir-fry gingerroot and garlic in hot oil for 15 seconds. Add red and green peppers; stir-fry for 3 to 4 minutes or till crisp-tender. Remove pepper mixture from the wok.

Add pork to the hot wok. Stir-fry for 2 to 3 minutes or till no pink remains. Push pork from the center of the wok.

Stir sauce. Add sauce to center of wok. Cook and stir till bubbly. Return pepper mixture to wok. Stir all ingredients together to coat with sauce. Cook and stir for 1 minute more or till heated through. Serve immediately over hot cooked noodles or rice. Makes 4 servings.

Nutrition information per serving: 292 calories, 18 g protein, 32 g carbohydrate, 10 g fat (3 g saturated fat), 63 mg cholesterol, 1,324 mg sodium, 494 mg potassium.

PORK AND PEAR STIR-FRY

Plum preserves, pears, and gingerroot give this delicious pork entrée its special sweetness.

1   pound pork tenderloin
½   cup plum preserves
3   tablespoons soy sauce
2   tablespoons lemon juice
1   tablespoon prepared horseradish
2   teaspoons cornstarch
½   teaspoon crushed red pepper
1   tablespoon cooking oil
2   teaspoons grated gingerroot
1   medium yellow or green sweet pepper,
     cut into julienne strips (1 cup)
1   medium pear, cored and sliced (1 cup)
⅓   cup sliced water chestnuts
1½ cups fresh pea pods, strings removed,
     or 4 ounces frozen pea pods,
     thawed
2   cups hot cooked rice

Trim fat from pork. Partially freeze pork. Thinly slice across grain into bite-size strips. Set aside.

For sauce, in a small bowl stir together preserves, soy sauce, lemon juice, horseradish, cornstarch, and crushed red pepper. Set aside.

Pour cooking oil into a wok or large skillet. (Add more oil as necessary during cooking.) Preheat over medium-high heat. Stir-fry gingerroot in hot oil for 15 seconds. Add sweet pepper and pear; stir-fry for 1½ minutes. Remove pear mixture from the wok.

Add *half* of the pork to the hot wok. Stir-fry for 2 to 3 minutes or till no pink remains. Remove pork from the wok. Repeat with remaining pork. Return all of the pork to the wok. Push pork from the center of the wok.

Stir sauce. Add sauce to the center of the wok. Cook and stir till slightly thickened and bubbly.

Return pear mixture to the wok. Add water chestnuts. Stir all ingredients together to coat with sauce. Cook and stir for 2 minutes. Top with pea pods. Cover and cook for 1 to 2 minutes more or till heated through. Serve immediately with hot cooked rice. Makes 4 servings.

Nutrition information per serving: 473 calories, 30 g protein, 70 g carbohydrate, 8 g fat (2 g saturated fat), 81 mg cholesterol, 884 mg sodium, 864 mg potassium.

POLYNESIAN STIR-FRY

This tangy sweet dish featuring a colorful mix of pineapple chunks and vegetables can be made with your choice of pork, lamb, or beef.

12 ounces lean boneless pork, lamb, or beef
3 tablespoons cider vinegar
3 tablespoons soy sauce
1 tablespoon brown sugar
1 teaspoon dry mustard
1 teaspoon grated gingerroot
¼ teaspoon pepper
1 8-ounce can pineapple chunks (juice pack)
2 teaspoons cornstarch
1 tablespoon cooking oil
1 medium onion, chopped (½ cup)
2 small zucchini, cut into julienne strips (1½ cups)
1 medium red or green sweet pepper, cut into 1-inch squares (1 cup)
2 cups hot cooked rice

Trim fat from pork, lamb, or beef. Partially freeze meat. Thinly slice across grain into bite-size strips. In a medium bowl stir together meat, vinegar, soy sauce, brown sugar, dry mustard, gingerroot, and pepper. Let stand for 15 minutes. Drain meat, reserving marinade. Set aside.

Drain pineapple, reserving juice. For sauce, in a small bowl stir together reserved pineapple juice, reserved marinade, and cornstarch. Set aside.

Pour cooking oil into a wok or large skillet. (Add more oil as necessary during cooking.) Preheat over medium-high heat. Stir-fry onion in hot oil for 2 minutes. Add zucchini and sweet pepper; stir-fry about 1½ minutes more or till vegetables are crisp-tender. Remove vegetables from the wok.

Add meat mixture to the hot wok. Stir-fry for 2 to 3 minutes or till no pink remains. Push meat from the center of the wok.

Stir sauce. Add sauce to the center of the wok. Cook and stir till thickened and bubbly. Return cooked vegetables to the wok. Add pineapple. Stir all ingredients together to coat with sauce. Cook and stir for 1 to 2 minutes more or till heated through. Serve immediately over hot cooked rice. Makes 4 servings.

Nutrition information per serving: 317 calories, 16 g protein, 42 g carbohydrate, 10 g fat (2 g saturated fat), 38 mg cholesterol, 806 mg sodium, 493 mg potassium.

PORK WITH APRICOTS AND PEPPERS

The zesty flavors of golden apricots, Dijon-style mustard, and fresh garlic lend themselves well to this non-Oriental pork stir-fry.

12 ounces lean boneless pork
½ cup dry white wine or chicken broth
⅓ cup dried apricots, cut into thin strips, or ⅓ cup mixed dried fruit bits
¼ cup water
2 teaspoons cornstarch
2 teaspoons sugar
1 teaspoon Dijon-style mustard
½ teaspoon dried oregano, crushed
¼ teaspoon salt
¼ teaspoon pepper
1 tablespoon cooking oil
2 cloves garlic, minced
1 medium onion, cut into thin wedges
1 large green sweet pepper, cut into 1-inch squares (1½ cups)
2 cups hot cooked rice

Trim fat from pork. Partially freeze pork. Thinly slice across grain into bite-size strips. Set aside.

For sauce, in a medium bowl combine wine or broth, apricots or dried fruit bits, water, cornstarch, sugar, mustard, oregano, salt, and pepper. Set aside.

Pour cooking oil into a wok or large skillet. (Add more oil as necessary during cooking.) Preheat over medium-high heat. Stir-fry garlic in hot oil for 15 seconds. Add onion; stir-fry for 1½ minutes. Add sweet pepper; stir-fry about 1½ minutes more or till crisp-tender. Remove vegetables from the wok.

Add pork to the hot wok. Stir-fry for 2 to 3 minutes or till no pink remains. Push pork from the center of the wok.

Stir sauce. Add sauce to the center of the wok. Cook and stir till thickened and bubbly. Return cooked vegetables to the wok. Stir all ingredients together to coat with sauce. Cook and stir for 1 to 2 minutes more or till heated through. Serve immediately with hot cooked rice. Makes 4 servings.

Nutrition information per serving: 331 calories, 16 g protein, 41 g carbohydrate, 10 g fat (3 g saturated fat), 38 mg cholesterol, 201 mg sodium, 561 mg potassium.

CURRIED CHICKEN SIAM

Unsweetened coconut milk, a common ingredient in Thai cuisine, is available in large supermarkets and Asian food stores. If you are unable to find it, use 1¼ cups milk mixed with ½ teaspoon coconut extract .

1 to 3 dried red Anaheim or California chili peppers
2 tablespoons snipped cilantro
1 teaspoon finely shredded lime peel
1 stalk lemon grass, cut into 2-inch pieces, or 1 teaspoon finely shredded lemon peel
1 teaspoon ground ginger
½ teaspoon salt
½ teaspoon ground nutmeg
½ teaspoon ground cumin
½ teaspoon ground coriander
12 ounces skinless, boneless chicken thighs
1 tablespoon cooking oil
4 cloves garlic, minced
2 medium onions, chopped (1 cup)
1¼ cups canned unsweetened coconut milk
1 8-ounce can sliced bamboo shoots, drained
1 medium red or green sweet pepper, cut into julienne strips (1 cup)
2 tablespoons snipped fresh basil or ¾ teaspoon dried basil, crushed
1 medium cucumber, halved lengthwise and sliced (optional)
2 cups hot cooked rice

Remove stems and seeds from chili peppers. Place in a medium bowl and cover with boiling water. Let stand about 15 minutes or till softeneds. Drain. Chop chili peppers. Set aside.

Meanwhile, for spice mixture, in a small bowl combine cilantro, lime peel, lemon grass or lemon peel, ginger, salt, nutmeg, cumin, and coriander. Set aside.

Rinse chicken and pat dry. Cut into 1-inch pieces. Set aside.

Pour cooking oil into a wok or large skillet. (Add more oil as necessary during cooking.) Preheat over medium-high heat. Stir-fry garlic in hot oil for 15 seconds. Add onions; stir-fry about 2 minutes or till crisp-tender. Add spice mixture; stir-fry for 2 minutes.

Add chicken; stir-fry for 3 to 4 minutes or till no pink remains. Discard lemon grass, if used.

Add coconut milk, bamboo shoots, sweet pepper, and the chili peppers. Cook and stir for 2 to 3 minutes more or till heated through. Stir in basil. If desired, arrange cucumber slices around the rim of a serving plate. Add meat mixture to plate. Serve immediately with hot cooked rice. Makes 4 servings.

Nutrition information per serving: 466 calories, 18 g protein, 34 g carbohydrate, 29 g fat (17 g saturated fat), 41 mg cholesterol, 339 mg sodium, 617 mg potassium.

HONEY-GINGER CHICKEN

The pungent aroma and pronounced flavor of Chinese five-spice powder—a blend of star anise, cloves, cinnamon, fennel, and Szechwan peppercorns—lends a distinctive taste to this poultry dish.

12 ounces skinless, boneless chicken thighs
2 tablespoons soy sauce
1 tablespoon honey
1 tablespoon dry sherry
1 teaspoon cornstarch
½ teaspoon five-spice powder
1 tablespoon cooking oil
2 teaspoons grated gingerroot
4 cloves garlic, thinly sliced
2 medium onions, cut into thin wedges
2 medium zucchini, halved lengthwise and sliced (2½ cups)
2 cups hot cooked rice
Julienne carrot strips (optional)

Rinse chicken and pat dry. Cut into thin bite-size strips. Set aside.

For sauce, in a small bowl stir together soy sauce, honey, sherry, cornstarch, and five-spice powder. Set aside.

Pour cooking oil into a wok or large skillet. (Add more oil as necessary during cooking.) Preheat over medium-high heat. Stir-fry gingerroot and garlic in hot oil for 15 seconds. Add onions; stir-fry for 3 to 4 minutes or till crisp-tender. Remove onion mixture from the wok. Add zucchini to the hot wok; stir-fry for 3 to 4 minutes or till crisp-tender. Remove zucchini from the wok.

Add chicken to the hot wok. Stir-fry for 2 to 3 minutes or till no pink remains. Push chicken from the center of the wok.

Stir sauce. Add sauce to the center of the wok. Cook and stir till thickened and bubbly. Return onion mixture and zucchini to wok. Stir all ingredients together to coat with sauce. Cook and stir for 1 to 2 minutes more or till heated through. Serve immediately with hot cooked rice. Sprinkle with carrots strips, if desired. Makes 4 servings.

Nutrition information per serving: 284 calories, 16 g protein, 35 g carbohydrate, 8 g fat (2 g saturated fat), 41 mg cholesterol, 561 mg sodium, 439 mg potassium.

CHICKEN PICCADILLO

Ask everyone to fill and roll their own tortillas right at the supper table—it makes less work for the cook and more fun for the family.

⅓ cup slivered almonds
½ cup picante sauce
2 teaspoons cornstarch
2 medium tomatoes, chopped (2 cups)
⅓ cup sliced pimiento-stuffed green olives
⅓ cup raisins
2 tablespoons snipped parsley
¼ teaspoon salt
¼ teaspoon pepper
¼ teaspoon ground cinnamon
⅛ teaspoon ground cloves
1½ pounds skinless, boneless chicken breast halves
12 8-inch flour tortillas
1 tablespoon cooking oil
3 cloves garlic, minced
2 medium onions, chopped (1 cup)
1 medium apple, cored and chopped (1 cup)
2 fresh, pickled, or canned jalapeño peppers, seeded and chopped (3 tablespoons)
12 leaves of leaf lettuce

Preheat a wok or 12-inch skillet over medium-high heat. Add almonds; stir-fry for 2 to 3 minutes or till golden. Remove almonds from the wok. Let wok cool.

For sauce, stir together picante sauce and cornstarch. Set aside. In a medium bowl stir together *undrained* tomatoes, olives, raisins, parsley, salt, pepper, cinnamon, cloves, and the almonds; set aside. Rinse chicken and pat dry. Cut into thin bite-size strips; set aside.

Stack tortillas; wrap in foil. Heat in a 350° oven for 10 minutes or till warm. *Or,* place tortillas, *half* at a time, between layers of microwave-safe paper towels. Micro-cook on 100% power (high) for 1½ to 2 minutes or till warm.

Pour oil into wok. (Add more oil as necessary during cooking.) Preheat over medium-high heat. Stir-fry garlic in hot oil for 15 seconds. Add onions, apple, and jalapeño peppers; stir-fry for 2 to 3 minutes or till crisp-tender. Remove apple mixture from the wok.

Add *half* of the chicken to the hot wok. Stir-fry for 2 to 3 minutes or till no pink remains. Remove chicken from the wok. Repeat with remaining chicken. Return all of the chicken and the apple mixture to wok. Push from center of wok.

Stir sauce. Add sauce and tomato mixture to the center of the wok. Cook and stir till thickened and bubbly. Stir all ingredients together to coat with sauce. Cook and stir for 2 minutes more. Place a lettuce leaf on each tortilla. Top with chicken mixture. Roll up tortilla. Serve immediately. Makes 6 servings.

Nutrition information per serving: 500 calories, 31 g protein, 61 g carbohydrate, 16 g fat (2 g saturated fat), 59 mg cholesterol, 974 mg sodium, 768 mg potassium.

KUNG PAO CHICKEN

Kung Pao means "guardian of the throne". Legend has it that this dish was named for a general—one of the throne's guardians—who woke up hungry in the middle of one night and commanded his personal chef to make him a snack. The chef found only leftover chicken and peanuts in the kitchen. Afraid to put leftovers before his master, the chef added lots of seasonings to mask the chicken's staleness and threw in the peanuts for good measure. The general loved it!

12 ounces skinless, boneless chicken
      breast halves
 1 tablespoon dry sherry
 1 teaspoon cornstarch
 ¼ cup water
 ¼ cup soy sauce
 4 teaspoons cornstarch
 1 tablespoon sugar
 1 teaspoon vinegar
     Few dashes bottled hot pepper sauce
 1 tablespoon cooking oil
 2 teaspoons grated gingerroot
 2 cloves garlic, minced
 6 green onions, cut into ½-inch pieces
      (1 cup)
 ½ cup dry roasted peanuts
 2 cups hot cooked rice
     Green onion fans (optional)

Rinse chicken and pat dry. Cut into ¾-inch pieces. In a medium bowl stir together chicken, sherry, and 1 teaspoon cornstarch. Let stand for 15 minutes.

For sauce, in a small bowl stir together water, soy sauce, 4 teaspoons cornstarch, sugar, vinegar, and hot pepper sauce. Set aside.

Pour cooking oil into a wok or large skillet. (Add more oil as necessary during cooking.) Preheat over medium-high heat. Stir-fry gingerroot and garlic in hot oil for 15 seconds. Add chicken mixture; stir-fry for 3 to 4 minutes or till no pink remains. Push chicken from the center of the wok.

Stir sauce. Add sauce to the center of the wok. Cook and stir till thickened and bubbly. Add green onion pieces and peanuts. Stir all ingredients together to coat with sauce. Cook and stir 1 to 2 minutes more or till heated through. Serve immediately with hot cooked rice. Garnish with green onion fans, if desired. Makes 4 servings.

Nutrition information per serving: 374 calories, 24 g protein, 35 g carbohydrate, 15 g fat (2 g saturated fat), 45 mg cholesterol, 1,220 mg sodium, 343 mg potassium.

CHICKEN PUTTANESCA

Stir-frying isn't just for Oriental cooking. This classic Italian recipe adapts readily to cooking in the wok.

12 ounces skinless, boneless chicken
    thighs or breast halves
1 16-ounce can tomatoes, cut up
¼ cup dry red wine or chicken broth
2 tablespoons tomato paste
2 tablespoons balsamic vinegar or red
    wine vinegar
1 tablespoon cornstarch
½ teaspoon salt
¼ teaspoon pepper
1 tablespoon cooking oil
2 cloves garlic, minced
8 ounces fresh medium mushrooms,
    quartered (about 3½ cups)
1 small onion, chopped (⅓ cup)
12 pitted ripe olives, halved
3 anchovy fillets, cut into ½-inch pieces
    (optional)
3 tablespoons snipped parsley
8 ounces spaghetti or other pasta,
    cooked and drained
    Parsley sprigs (optional)

Rinse chicken and pat dry. Cut into thin bite-size strips. Set aside.

For sauce, in a bowl stir together *undrained* tomatoes, wine or broth, tomato paste, vinegar, cornstarch, salt, and pepper. Set aside.

Pour cooking oil into a wok or large skillet. (Add more oil as necessary during cooking.) Preheat over medium-high heat. Stir-fry garlic in hot oil for 15 seconds. Add mushrooms and onion; stir-fry for 1 to 2 minutes or till onion is crisp-tender. Remove mushroom mixture from the wok.

Add chicken to the hot wok. Stir-fry for 2 to 3 minutes or till no pink remains. Push chicken from the center of the wok.

Stir sauce. Add sauce to the center of the wok. Cook and stir till thickened and bubbly. Return mushroom mixture to the wok. Add olives, anchovies (if desired), and parsley. Stir all ingredients together to coat with sauce. Cook and stir for 1 to 2 minutes more or till heated through. Serve immediately over hot cooked pasta. Garnish with parsley sprigs, if desired. Makes 4 servings.

Nutrition information per serving: 432 calories, 23 g protein, 59 g carbohydrate, 11 g fat (2 g saturated fat), 41 mg cholesterol, 570 mg sodium, 751 mg potassium.

FRAGRANT SPICED CHICKEN

Given Malaysia's location in the island crossroads of Southeast Asia and its importance in the spice trade, it's no surprise that the cuisine embraces a mix of cultures and uses a wealth of spices. This Malaysian dish shows a blend of both Indian and Asian influences.

12 ounces skinless, boneless chicken thighs
2 teaspoons ground coriander
1½ teaspoons ground cumin
1 teaspoon ground turmeric
1 teaspoon ground nutmeg
¾ teaspoon ground cinnamon
¼ teaspoon ground red pepper
¼ teaspoon ground cloves
⅔ cup water
¼ cup cider vinegar
3 tablespoons sugar
1 tablespoon cornstarch
½ teaspoon salt
1 tablespoon cooking oil
1 tablespoon grated gingerroot
4 cloves garlic, minced
2 medium onions, cut into thin wedges
1 medium red or green sweet pepper, cut into strips (1 cup)
½ stalk lemon grass, cut into 2-inch pieces, or ½ teaspoon finely shredded lemon peel
2 cups hot cooked couscous or rice
3 tablespoons coarsely chopped roasted peanuts
Fresh rosemary sprigs (optional)

Rinse chicken and pat dry. Cut into 1-inch pieces. In a medium bowl combine coriander, cumin, turmeric, nutmeg, cinnamon, ground red pepper, and cloves. Add chicken; stir to coat. Set aside.

For sauce, in a small bowl stir together water, vinegar, sugar, cornstarch, and salt. Set aside.

Pour cooking oil into a wok or large skillet. (Add more oil as necessary during cooking.) Preheat over medium-high heat. Stir-fry gingerroot and garlic in hot oil for 15 seconds. Add onions, sweet pepper, and lemon grass or lemon peel; stir-fry for 2 to 3 minutes or till vegetables are crisp-tender. Remove vegetables from the wok. Discard lemon grass, if used.

Add chicken mixture to the hot wok. Stir-fry chicken for 3 to 4 minutes or till no pink remains, scraping the bottom of the wok constantly to prevent spices from sticking. Push chicken from the center of the wok.

Stir sauce. Add sauce to the center of the wok. Cook and stir till thickened and bubbly. Return cooked vegetables to the wok. Stir all ingredients together to coat with sauce. Cook and stir for 1 to 2 minutes more or till heated through. Serve immediately with hot cooked couscous or rice. Sprinkle with peanuts. Garnish with fresh rosemary, if desired. Makes 4 servings.

Nutrition information per serving: 350 calories, 19 g protein, 44 g carbohydrate, 12 g fat (2 g saturated fat), 41 mg cholesterol, 456 mg sodium, 411 mg potassium.

CHICKEN AND APPLE STIR-FRY

This sweet-spiced dish includes an array of colorful peppers, plus dried mushrooms, crunchy almonds, and crisp, tart apple slices.

  6 dried mushrooms (1 cup), such as shiitake or wood ear mushrooms
 12 ounces skinless, boneless chicken breast halves or turkey breast tenderloin steaks
 ¾ cup cold water
  3 tablespoons frozen orange, apple, or pineapple juice concentrate, thawed
  2 tablespoons soy sauce
  2 teaspoons cornstarch
 ¼ teaspoon ground ginger
 ¼ teaspoon ground cinnamon
 ⅛ to ¼ teaspoon ground red pepper
 ¼ cup sliced or slivered almonds
  1 tablespoon cooking oil
  2 medium green, red, orange, and/or yellow sweet peppers, cut into thin 2-inch strips (2 cups)
  2 medium apples, thinly sliced (2 cups)
  2 cups hot cooked brown rice

In a small bowl cover mushrooms with warm water. Let soak for 30 minutes. Rinse and squeeze mushrooms to drain thoroughly. Discard stems. Thinly slice mushrooms. Set aside.

Meanwhile, rinse chicken or turkey and pat dry. Cut into 1-inch pieces. Set aside.

For sauce, in a small bowl stir together cold water, juice concentrate, soy sauce, cornstarch, ginger, cinnamon, and red pepper. Set aside.

Preheat a wok or large skillet over medium-high heat. Add almonds; stir-fry for 2 to 3 minutes or till golden. Remove almonds from the wok. Let wok cool.

Pour cooking oil into the cooled wok. (Add more oil as necessary during cooking.) Add mushrooms, sweet peppers, and apples; stir-fry for 1 to 2 minutes or till peppers and apples are crisp-tender. Remove apple mixture from the wok.

Add chicken or turkey to the hot wok; stir-fry for 3 to 4 minutes or till no pink remains. Push chicken or turkey from the center of the wok.

Stir sauce. Add sauce to the center of the wok. Cook and stir till thickened and bubbly. Return apple mixture to the wok. Stir all ingredients together to coat with sauce. Cook and stir 1 to 2 minutes more or till heated through. Stir in toasted almonds. Serve immediately over hot cooked brown rice. Makes 4 servings.

Nutrition information per serving: 370 calories, 22 g protein, 48 g carbohydrate, 11 g fat (2 g saturated fat), 45 mg cholesterol, 563 mg sodium, 560 mg potassium.

ASIAN VINEGAR CHICKEN

Vietnamese dishes like this one show a marked similarity to Chinese cuisine. The differences are subtle but are noted by the use of fish sauce instead of soy sauce in this sweet-and-sour recipe.

8 dried mushrooms (1⅓ cups), such as shiitake or wood ear mushrooms
1 pound skinless, boneless chicken breast halves
4 green onions, sliced (½ cup)
1 stalk lemon grass, cut into 2-inch lengths, or 1 teaspoon finely shredded lemon peel
½ teaspoon salt
½ teaspoon pepper
¼ cup water
2 tablespoons cider vinegar or white vinegar
2 teaspoons grated gingerroot
1 tablespoon cooking oil
6 cloves garlic, minced
4 cups sliced bok choy
1 medium onion, chopped (½ cup)
1 to 2 tablespoons fish sauce
1 teaspoon sugar
2 cups hot cooked Chinese egg noodles or fine egg noodles
1 small red sweet pepper, cut into bite-size strips (optional)

In a small bowl cover mushrooms with warm water. Let soak for 30 minutes. Rinse well and squeeze to drain thoroughly. Thinly slice mushroom caps. Discard stems. Set sliced caps aside.

Meanwhile rinse chicken and pat dry. Cut into thin bite-size strips. In a medium bowl stir together green onions, lemon grass or lemon peel, salt, and pepper. Stir in chicken. Let stand for 15 minutes.

For sauce, in a small bowl stir together water, vinegar, and gingerroot. Set aside.

Pour cooking oil into a wok or large skillet. (Add more oil as necessary during cooking.) Preheat over medium-high heat. Stir-fry garlic in hot oil for 15 seconds. Add bok choy and onion; stir-fry for 2 to 3 minutes or till crisp-tender. Remove bok choy mixture from the wok.

Add *half* of the chicken mixture to the hot wok. Stir-fry for 2 to 3 minutes or till no pink remains. Remove chicken from the wok. Repeat with remaining chicken mixture. Return all chicken to the wok. Discard lemon grass, if used. Push chicken from the center of the wok.

Add sauce to the center of the wok. Cover and cook for 1 minute. Uncover wok. Add fish sauce, sugar, and mushrooms. Cook and stir for 2 minutes or till sauce is slightly reduced. Return bok choy mixture to the wok. Stir all ingredients together to coat with sauce. Cook and stir for 1 to 2 minutes more or till heated through. Serve immediately over hot cooked noodles. Sprinkle with red sweet pepper strips, if desired. Makes 4 to 5 servings.

Nutrition information per serving: 314 calories, 27 g protein, 33 g carbohydrate, 8 g fat (2 g saturated fat), 87 mg cholesterol, 467 mg sodium, 425 mg potassium.

CHICKEN WITH TOMATO AND EGGPLANT

Although any pasta can be used, we chose mafalada—junior-size ribbons of ruffled-edge lasagna—to serve with this hearty, well-seasoned dish.

12 ounces skinless, boneless chicken breast halves
1 14½-ounce can tomato wedges
1 8-ounce can tomato sauce
¼ cup dry red wine
1 tablespoon cornstarch
½ teaspoon dried oregano, crushed
½ teaspoon dried basil, crushed
¼ teaspoon salt
1 tablespoon cooking oil
2 cloves garlic, minced
1 medium green sweet pepper, cut into strips (1 cup)
1 small onion, chopped (⅓ cup)
1 small eggplant, peeled and cut into ¾-inch cubes (about 3 cups)
8 ounces mafalada or other pasta, cooked and drained
¼ cup grated Parmesan cheese

Rinse chicken and pat dry. Cut chicken into 1-inch pieces. Set aside.

Drain tomatoes, reserving juice. For sauce, in a small bowl stir together reserved tomato juice, tomato sauce, wine, cornstarch, oregano, basil, and salt. Set aside.

Pour cooking oil into a wok or large skillet. (Add more oil as necessary during cooking.) Preheat over medium-high heat. Stir-fry garlic in hot oil for 15 seconds. Add green pepper and onion; stir-fry for 2 minutes or till crisp-tender. Remove pepper mixture from the wok.

Add eggplant to the hot wok; stir-fry for 3 to 4 minutes or till just tender. Remove eggplant from the wok.

Add chicken to the hot wok. Stir-fry for 2 to 3 minutes or till no pink remains. Push chicken from the center of the wok.

Stir sauce. Add sauce to the center of the wok. Cook and stir till thickened and bubbly. Return cooked pepper mixture and eggplant to the wok. Add tomato wedges. Stir all ingredients together to coat with sauce. Cook and stir for 1 to 2 minutes more or till heated through. Serve immediately over hot cooked pasta. Sprinkle with Parmesan cheese. Makes 4 servings.

Nutrition information per serving: 472 calories, 29 g protein, 65 g carbohydrate, 9 g fat (3 g saturated fat), 50 mg cholesterol, 827 mg sodium, 946 mg potassium.

COUNTRY CHICKEN STIR-FRY

For a savory solution to the dinner question, sample this stir-fried stew. It features chunks of carrots, potatoes, and chicken in a simple, herb-seasoned sauce, and it cooks in just minutes.

4	medium potatoes, cut into ¾-inch pieces
4	medium carrots, thinly sliced (2 cups)
12	ounces skinless, boneless chicken breast halves
¾	cup water
1	teaspoon cornstarch
1	teaspoon instant chicken bouillon granules
1	teaspoon dried thyme, crushed
½	teaspoon salt
⅛	teaspoon pepper
1	tablespoon cooking oil
1	large onion, chopped (1 cup)
3	tablespoons snipped parsley

In a medium saucepan precook potatoes and carrots, covered, in enough boiling water to cover about 10 minutes or just till tender. Drain. Set aside.

Rinse chicken and pat dry. Cut into thin bite-size strips. Set aside.

For sauce, in a small bowl stir together water, cornstarch, bouillon granules, thyme, salt, and pepper. Set aside.

Pour cooking oil into a wok or large skillet. (Add more oil as necessary during cooking.) Preheat over medium-high heat. Stir-fry onions in hot oil for 2 minutes or till crisp-tender.

Add chicken to the hot wok; stir-fry for 2 to 3 minutes or till no pink remains. Push chicken from the center of the wok.

Stir sauce. Add sauce to the center of the wok. Cook and stir till thickened and bubbly. Add cooked potatoes and carrots. Stir all ingredients together to coat with sauce. Cover and cook for 2 minutes more or till heated through. Stir in parsley. Serve immediately. Makes 4 servings.

Nutrition information per serving: 323 calories, 21 g protein, 47 g carbohydrate, 6 g fat (1 g saturated fat), 45 mg cholesterol, 583 mg sodium, 986 mg potassium.

SZECHWAN-STYLE CHICKEN
Skip the Chinese take-out and create your own delicious Oriental meal in just minutes at home.

1   pound skinless, boneless chicken breast halves

⅓   cup teriyaki sauce

3   tablespoons Szechwan spicy stir-fry sauce

2   teaspoons cornstarch

1   tablespoon cooking oil

1   large onion, chopped (1 cup)

3   cups chopped bok choy

1   cup broccoli flowerets

1   medium red sweet pepper, cut into strips (1 cup)

2   cups fresh pea pods, strings removed, or one 6-ounce package frozen pea pods, thawed

1   14-ounce can whole baby sweet corn, drained and halved crosswise

1   7-ounce jar whole straw mushrooms, drained

3   cups hot cooked rice noodles or rice

Rinse chicken and pat dry. Cut into thin bite-size strips. Set aside.

For sauce, in a small bowl stir together teriyaki sauce, stir-fry sauce, and cornstarch. Set aside.

Pour cooking oil into a wok or large skillet. (Add more oil as necessary during cooking.) Preheat over medium-high heat. Stir-fry onion in hot oil for 2 minutes. Add bok choy, broccoli, and sweet pepper; stir-fry for 1 minute. Add fresh pea pods (if using); stir-fry for 1 to 2 minutes more or till vegetables are crisp-tender. Remove vegetables from the wok.

Add *half* of the chicken to the hot wok. Stir-fry for 2 to 3 minutes or till no pink remains. Remove chicken from the wok. Repeat with remaining chicken. Return all chicken to the wok. Push chicken from the center of the wok.

Stir sauce. Add sauce to the center of the wok. Cook and stir till thickened and bubbly. Return cooked vegetables to the wok. Add corn, mushrooms, and thawed frozen pea pods (if using). Stir all ingredients together to coat with sauce. Cook and stir about 1 minute more or till heated through. Serve immediately over hot cooked rice noodles or rice. Makes 6 servings.

Nutrition information per serving: 260 calories, 22 g protein, 32 g carbohydrate, 5 g fat (1 g saturated fat), 40 mg cholesterol, 1,045 mg sodium, 783 mg potassium.

CHICKEN WITH LONG BEANS AND WALNUTS

Yard-long beans, more commonly called Chinese long beans, can grow to a length of 18 inches, but they cook in much less time than regular green beans. Look for them in Asian markets and some supermarkets.

12 ounces skinless, boneless chicken
   breast halves
2 tablespoons hoisin sauce
1 tablespoon soy sauce
1 tablespoon water
½ teaspoon sugar
8 ounces fresh Chinese long beans, cut
   into 4-inch lengths, or 8 ounces
   fresh whole green beans
1 tablespoon cooking oil
3 cloves garlic, minced
1 medium onion, cut into thin wedges
½ cup coarsely broken walnuts
2 cups hot cooked rice

Rinse chicken and pat dry. Cut into 1-inch pieces. Set aside.

For sauce, in a small bowl stir together hoisin sauce, soy sauce, water, and sugar. Set aside.

In a medium saucepan pre-cook long beans, covered, in small amount of boiling water for 3 to 5 minutes (cook whole green beans about 10 minutes) or till crisp-tender. Drain. Set aside.

Pour cooking oil into a wok or large skillet. (Add more oil as necessary during cooking.) Preheat over medium-high heat. Stir-fry garlic in hot oil for 15 seconds. Add onion; stir-fry about 3 minutes or till crisp-tender. Remove onion mixture from the wok.

Add walnuts to the hot wok; stir-fry for 2 to 3 minutes or till golden. Remove walnuts from the wok.

Add chicken to the hot wok; stir-fry for 3 to 4 minutes or till no pink remains. Return onion mixture and walnuts to the wok. Add beans.

Stir sauce. Add sauce to the wok. Stir all ingredients together to coat with sauce. Cook and stir for 1 to 2 minutes more or till heated through. Serve immediately over hot cooked rice. Makes 4 servings.

Nutrition information per serving: 363 calories, 23 g protein, 34 g carbohydrate, 16 g fat (2 g saturated fat), 45 mg cholesterol, 817 mg sodium, 482 mg potassium.

TURKEY-APRICOT STIR-FRY

Tangy apricots make this sweet-and-sour entrée pleasantly different from other stir-fries.

12 ounces turkey breast tenderloin steaks
½ cup apricot or peach nectar
3 tablespoons soy sauce
2 tablespoons rice vinegar or white
     vinegar
1 tablespoon cornstarch
¼ teaspoon ground red pepper
½ cup dried apricot halves, cut in half
1 tablespoon cooking oil
1 small onion, chopped (⅓ cup)
2 cups fresh pea pods, strings removed,
     or one 6-ounce package frozen pea
     pods, thawed
1 small red or green sweet pepper, cut
     into 1-inch pieces
2 cups hot cooked couscous or rice

Rinse turkey and pat dry. Cut into thin bite-size strips. Set aside.

For sauce, in a small bowl stir together nectar, soy sauce, vinegar, cornstarch, and ground red pepper; stir in apricots. Set aside.

Pour cooking oil into a wok or large skillet. (Add more oil as necessary during cooking.) Preheat over medium-high heat. Stir-fry onion in hot oil for 1 minute. Add fresh pea pods (if using) and sweet pepper; stir-fry 1 to 2 minutes more or till crisp-tender. Remove vegetables from the wok.

Add turkey to the hot wok. Stir-fry for 2 to 3 minutes or till no pink remains. Push turkey from the center of the wok.

Stir sauce. Add sauce to center of the wok. Cook and stir till thickened and bubbly. Return cooked vegetables to wok. Stir in thawed frozen pea pods (if using). Stir all ingredients together to coat with sauce. Cook and stir 1 minute more or till heated through. Serve immediately over hot cooked couscous or rice. Makes 4 servings.

Nutrition information per serving: 325 calories, 23 g protein, 46 g carbohydrate, 6 g fat (1 g saturated fat), 37 mg cholesterol, 817 mg sodium, 699 mg potassium.

CREAMY TURKEY DIJON

Mustard, onion, and garlic add zest to this up scale version of an old favorite—turkey à la king. Serve it over noodles or fettuccine, and it becomes a classy pasta dish everyone will enjoy.

12	ounces turkey breast tenderloin steaks
2	tablespoons all-purpose flour
2	tablespoons Dijon-style mustard
2	tablespoons dry white wine
½	teaspoon salt
⅛	teaspoon pepper
1	cup half-and-half or light cream
1	tablespoon cooking oil
1	clove garlic, minced
1	medium red or green sweet pepper, cut into julienne strips (1 cup)
1	medium onion, chopped (½ cup)
1½	cups sliced fresh mushrooms
¾	cup frozen peas, thawed
2	cups hot cooked noodles or fettuccine
	Fresh whole mushrooms (optional)
	Fresh basil sprigs (optional)

Rinse turkey and pat dry. Cut into thin bite-size strips. Set aside.

For sauce, in a small bowl stir together flour, mustard, wine, salt, and pepper till smooth. Slowly stir in half-and-half or light cream till well mixed. Set aside.

Pour cooking oil into a wok or large skillet. (Add more oil as necessary during cooking.) Preheat over medium-high heat. Stir-fry garlic in hot oil for 15 seconds. Add sweet pepper and onion; stir-fry for 2 minutes. Add sliced mushrooms; stir-fry for 2 minutes more or till crisp-tender. Remove vegetables from the wok.

Add turkey to the hot wok. Stir-fry for 2 to 3 minutes or till no pink remains. Push turkey from the center of the wok.

Stir sauce. Add sauce to the center of the wok. Cook and stir till thickened and bubbly. Return cooked vegetables to the wok. Add thawed peas. Stir all ingredients together to coat with sauce. Cook and stir for 1 to 2 minutes more or till heated through. Serve immediately over hot cooked noodles or fettuccine. Garnish with whole mushrooms and fresh basil, if desired. Makes 4 servings.

Nutrition information per serving: 463 calories, 28 g protein, 52 g carbohydrate, 15 g fat (6 g saturated fat), 108 mg cholesterol, 553 mg sodium, 521 mg potassium.

PINEAPPLE-ORANGE GINGER TURKEY

This easy-to-fix Polynesian-style dish capitalizes on the tangy-sweet flavors of pineapple and orange juice concentrate plus a generous amount of fresh ginger.

1   pound turkey breast tenderloin steaks
2   tablespoons soy sauce
2   tablespoons dry sherry
½   of a 6-ounce can (⅓ cup) frozen orange juice concentrate, thawed
2   tablespoons soy sauce
1   tablespoon water
2   teaspoons cornstarch
½   teaspoon sugar
1   tablespoon cooking oil
2   to 3 teaspoons grated gingerroot
1   medium red or green sweet pepper, cut into bite-size strips (1 cup)
1   8-ounce can pineapple chunks, (juice pack) drained
2   cups hot cooked rice
    Orange slices (optional)
    Fresh rosemary (optional)

Rinse turkey and pat dry. Cut into thin bite-size strips. In a medium bowl stir together turkey, 2 tablespoons soy sauce, and sherry. Cover and refrigerate for 30 minutes to 1 hour.

For sauce, in a small bowl stir together orange juice concentrate, 2 tablespoons soy sauce, water, cornstarch, and sugar. Set aside.

Pour cooking oil into a wok or large skillet. (Add more oil as necessary during cooking.) Preheat over medium-high heat. Stir-fry gingerroot in hot oil for 15 seconds. Add pepper strips; stir-fry for 1 to 2 minutes or till crisp-tender. Remove pepper strips from the wok.

Add *half* of the turkey mixture to the hot wok. Stir-fry for 2 to 3 minutes or till no pink remains. Remove turkey from the wok. Repeat with remaining turkey mixture. Return all turkey to the wok. Push turkey from the center of the wok.

Stir sauce. Add sauce to the center of the wok. Cook and stir till thickened and bubbly. Return pepper strips to the wok. Add pineapple. Stir all ingredients together to coat with sauce. Cook and stir about 1 minute more or till heated through. Serve immediately with hot cooked rice. Garnish with orange slices and rosemary, if desired. Makes 4 servings.

Nutrition information per serving: 352 calories, 25 g protein, 46 g carbohydrate, 6 g fat (1 g saturated fat), 50 mg cholesterol, 1,077 mg sodium, 555 mg potassium.

WARM TURKEY SALAD

Strips of tender turkey breast marinate in a trio of Chinese flavors—soy sauce, garlic, and ginger—in this refreshing main-dish salad.

12 ounces turkey breast tenderloin steaks
 3 tablespoons soy sauce
 2 cloves garlic, minced
1½ teaspoons grated gingerroot
 1 teaspoon sugar
    Few dashes bottled hot pepper sauce
 3 tablespoons cooking oil
 2 tablespoons lemon juice
 ½ teaspoon toasted sesame oil
 2 cups fresh green beans, cut into 1-
      inch pieces, or one 9-ounce package
      frozen cut green beans, thawed
 1 tablespoon cooking oil
 2 teaspoons sesame seed
 1 cup thinly sliced radishes
 ½ of a large cucumber, peeled and
      chopped (¾ cup)
 4 green onions, sliced (½ cup)
 1 stalk celery, thinly sliced (½ cup)
 6 cups torn mixed salad greens
    Whole radishes (optional)

Rinse turkey and pat dry. Cut into thin bite-size strips. In a medium bowl stir together turkey, soy sauce, garlic, gingerroot, sugar, and hot pepper sauce. Cover and refrigerate for 1 to 2 hours.

For dressing, in a small bowl stir together 3 tablespoons cooking oil, lemon juice, and sesame oil. Set aside.

If using fresh green beans, precook in a medium saucepan in small amount of boiling water for 10 minutes. Drain; set aside.

Pour 1 tablespoon cooking oil into a wok or 12-inch skillet. (Add more oil as necessary during cooking.) Preheat over medium-high heat. Stir-fry green beans in hot oil for 3 minutes or till crisp-tender. Remove green beans from the wok.

Add turkey mixture to the hot wok. Sprinkle with sesame seed. Stir-fry for 2 to 3 minutes or till no pink remains in turkey. Remove the wok from the heat.

Return green beans to the wok. Add sliced radishes, cucumber, green onions, celery, and dressing. Stir all ingredients together to coat with dressing. Toss with mixed greens. Serve immediately. Garnish with whole radishes, if desired. Makes 4 servings.

Nutrition information per serving: 275 calories, 20 g protein, 12 g carbohydrate, 17 g fat (3 g saturated fat), 37 mg cholesterol, 863 mg sodium, 757 mg potassium.

TURKEY TETRAZZINI

Tetrazzini is a quick supper when cooked in a wok—there's plenty of room for tossing the spaghetti with the meat, mushrooms, and creamy sauce.

12 ounces turkey breast tenderloin steaks
1⅔ cups milk
2 tablespoons all-purpose flour
2 teaspoons instant chicken bouillon granules
⅛ teaspoon pepper
¼ cup slivered almonds
1 tablespoon cooking oil
1 cup sliced fresh mushrooms
2 green onions, sliced (¼ cup)
2 tablespoons dry white wine, dry sherry, or milk
4 ounces thin spaghetti, cooked and drained
¼ cup finely shredded Parmesan cheese
2 tablespoons snipped parsley
   Tomato slices (optional)
   Parsley sprigs (optional)

Rinse turkey and pat dry. Cut into thin bite-size strips. Set aside.

For sauce, in a small bowl stir together 1⅔ cup milk, flour, bouillon granules, and pepper till smooth. Set aside.

Preheat a wok or large skillet over medium-high heat. Add almonds; stir-fry for 2 to 3 minutes or till golden. Remove almonds from the wok. Let wok cool.

Pour cooking oil into cooled wok. (Add more oil as necessary during cooking.) Preheat over medium-high heat. Stir-fry mushrooms and green onions in hot oil for 1 to 2 minutes or till just tender. Remove mushroom mixture from the wok.

Add turkey to the hot wok; stir-fry for 3 to 4 minutes or till no pink remains. Push turkey from the center of the wok.

Stir sauce. Add sauce to the center of the wok. Cook and stir till thickened and bubbly. Cook and stir for 2 minutes more. Stir in wine. Return mushroom mixture to the wok. Add cooked spaghetti, Parmesan cheese, and parsley. Toss all ingredients together to coat with sauce. Cook and stir for 1 to 2 minutes more or till heated through. Serve immediately. Sprinkle with toasted almonds. Garnish with tomato slices and parsley sprigs, if desired. Makes 4 servings.

Nutrition information per serving: 376 calories, 28 g protein, 34 g carbohydrate, 13 g fat (4 g saturated fat), 50 mg cholesterol, 637 mg sodium, 504 mg potassium.

TURKEY FAJITAS

Stir-frying makes short work of preparing the stuffing for these popular Tex-Mex sandwich roll-ups.

12	ounces turkey breast tenderloin steaks
¼	cup soy sauce
2	tablespoons sugar
2	tablespoons lemon juice
1	tablespoon cornstarch
¼	teaspoon crushed red pepper
4	8-inch flour tortillas
1	tablespoon cooking oil
3	cloves garlic, minced
3	medium green, red, and/or yellow sweet peppers, cut into thin strips (3 cups)
1	medium onion, chopped (½ cup)

Rinse turkey and pat dry. Cut into thin bite-size strips. Set aside.

For sauce, in a small bowl stir together soy sauce, sugar, lemon juice, cornstarch, and crushed red pepper. Set aside.

Stack tortillas; wrap in foil. Heat in a 350° oven for 10 minutes or till warm. *Or,* place tortillas, *half* at a time, between layers of microwave-safe paper towels. Micro-cook on 100% power (high) for 1½ to 2 minutes or till warm.

Pour cooking oil into a wok or large skillet. (Add more oil as necessary during cooking.) Preheat over medium-high heat. Stir-fry garlic in hot oil for 15 seconds. Add sweet peppers and onion; stir-fry for 2 to 3 minutes or till crisp-tender. Remove vegetables from the wok.

Add turkey to the hot wok. Stir-fry for 2 to 3 minutes or till no pink remains. Push turkey from the center of the wok.

Stir sauce. Add sauce to the center of the wok. Cook and stir till thickened and bubbly. Return cooked vegetables to the wok. Stir all ingredients together to coat with sauce. Cook and stir about 1 minute more or till heated through. Spoon turkey mixture onto warm tortillas and roll up. Serve immediately. Makes 4 servings.

Nutrition information per serving: 336 calories, 22 g protein, 45 g carbohydrate, 8 g fat (1 g saturated fat), 37 mg cholesterol, 1,236 mg sodium, 625 mg potassium.

TUNA WITH VEGETABLES AND LINGUINE

Fresh tuna, and other firm-fleshed fish, is well suited to stir-frying because it holds its shape well while being quickly cooked and stirred.

12	ounces fresh or frozen tuna steaks or fillets (1 inch thick)
½	cup dry white wine
1	teaspoon dried thyme, crushed
½	teaspoon salt
⅛	to ¼ teaspoon crushed red pepper
1	tablespoon cooking oil
2	cloves garlic, minced
2	cups broccoli flowerets
1	large red or green sweet pepper, cut into julienne stripes (1½ cups)
8	ounces linguine, cooked and drained
¾	cup finely shredded Romano or Parmesan cheese

Thaw fish, if frozen. Cut into 1-inch cubes. Discard any skin and bones. Set aside.

For sauce, in a small bowl stir together wine, thyme, salt, and crushed red pepper. Set aside.

Pour cooking oil into a wok or large skillet. (Add more oil as necessary during cooking.) Preheat over medium-high heat. Stir-fry garlic in hot oil for 15 seconds. Add broccoli; stir-fry for 2 minutes. Add sweet pepper; stir-fry for 1 to 2 minutes more or till vegetables are crisp-tender. Remove vegetables from the wok.

Add tuna to the hot wok. Stir-fry for 3 to 6 minutes or till tuna flakes easily, being careful not to break up pieces. Return cooked vegetables to the wok.

Stir sauce. Add sauce to the wok. Add cooked linguine. Gently toss all ingredients together to coat with sauce. Cook and stir 1 to 2 minutes more or till heated through. Remove from heat. Serve immediately. Sprinkle each serving with Romano or Parmesan cheese. Makes 4 servings.

Nutrition information per serving: 512 calories, 38 g protein, 51 g carbohydrate, 15 g fat (5 g saturated fat), 57 mg cholesterol, 574 mg sodium, 517 mg potassium.

SWORDFISH IN CHILI SAUCE

Hot bean sauce or paste is a pungent blend of fermented soy beans and hot chili peppers. It adds the heat to spicy Asian dishes such as this one. Look for hot bean sauce or paste in Oriental grocery stores, specialty shops, or large supermarkets.

12 ounces fresh or frozen swordfish or
   tuna steaks (1 inch thick)
3 tablespoons dry sherry
½ teaspoon salt
½ cup water
2 to 3 teaspoons hot bean sauce or hot
   bean paste
2 teaspoons sugar
1 teaspoon instant chicken bouillon
   granules
1 tablespoon cooking oil
1 tablespoon grated gingerroot
1 medium onion, cut into thin wedges
1 medium red sweet pepper, cut into
   julienne strips (1 cup)
1 medium yellow or green sweet pepper,
   cut into julienne strips (1 cup)
1 8-ounce can sliced bamboo shoots,
   drained
4 green onions, cut into 1-inch pieces
2 cups hot cooked rice

Thaw fish, if frozen. Cut into 1-inch cubes. Discard any skin and bones. In a medium bowl stir together fish, sherry, and salt. Let stand for 15 minutes. Drain. Set aside.

For sauce, in a small bowl stir together water, bean sauce or paste, sugar, and bouillon granules. Set aside.

Pour cooking oil into a wok or large skillet. (Add more oil as necessary during cooking.) Preheat over medium-high heat. Stir-fry gingerroot in hot oil for 15 seconds. Add onion; stir-fry for 2 minutes. Add red and yellow sweet peppers; stir-fry for 1 to 2 minutes or till vegetables are crisp-tender. Remove vegetables from the wok.

Add fish to the hot wok. Stir-fry for 3 to 6 minutes or till fish flakes easily, being careful not to break up pieces. Push fish from the center of the wok.

Stir sauce. Add sauce to the center of the wok. Cook and stir till bubbly. Return cooked vegetables to the wok. Add bamboo shoots and green onions. Gently stir all ingredients together to coat with sauce. Cook and stir for 1 to 2 minutes more or till heated through. Serve immediately over hot cooked rice. Makes 4 servings.

Nutrition information per serving: 294 calories, 21 g protein, 33 g carbohydrate, 7 g fat (2 g saturated fat), 34 mg cholesterol, 737 mg sodium, 468 mg potassium.

FISH CREOLE

For a refreshingly light entrée, stir-fry fish with the classic flavors of New Orleans—green pepper, celery, onion, and tomatoes.

1   pound fresh or frozen swordfish,
       sea bass, tuna, or tile fish steaks
       (1 inch thick)
1   16-ounce can tomatoes, cut up
½   teaspoon salt
½   teaspoon sugar
⅛   to ¼ teaspoon ground red pepper
1   tablespoon cooking oil
1   medium onion, chopped (½ cup)
1   stalk celery, thinly sliced (½ cup)
1   medium green sweet pepper, cut into
       2-inch strips (1 cup)
2   tablespoons snipped parsley
2   cups hot cooked rice

Thaw fish, if frozen. Cut into 1-inch cubes. Discard any skin and bones. Set aside.

In a small bowl stir together *undrained* tomatoes, salt, sugar, and ground red pepper. Set aside.

Pour cooking oil into a wok or large skillet. (Add more oil as necessary during cooking.) Preheat over medium-high heat. Stir-fry onion and celery in hot oil for 2 minutes. Add sweet pepper; stir-fry about 2 minutes more or till vegetables are crisp-tender. Remove vegetables from the wok.

Add *half* of the fish to the hot wok. Stir-fry for 3 to 6 minutes or till fish flakes easily, being careful not to break up pieces. Remove fish from the wok. Repeat with remaining fish. Remove all of the fish from the wok; set aside.

Stir tomato mixture. Add tomato mixture to the hot wok. Return cooked vegetables to the wok. Stir all ingredients together. Cook and stir about 3 minutes or till slightly thickened. Add parsley. Gently stir in fish. Cook for 1 to 2 minutes more or till heated through. Serve immediately in bowls over hot cooked rice. Makes 4 servings.

Nutrition information per serving: 311 calories, 26 g protein, 31 g carbohydrate, 9 g fat (2 g saturated fat), 45 mg cholesterol, 569 mg sodium, 723 mg potassium.

SALMON IN GINGER-LIME SAUCE

Serve this zesty salmon dish as a warm salad on a bed of crisp, shredded lettuce.

12 ounces fresh or frozen salmon fillets
     or steaks (1 inch thick)
½ cup water
1 teaspoon finely shredded lime peel
2 tablespoons lime juice
2 tablespoons dry white wine
1 tablespoon cornstarch
2 teaspoons soy sauce
1 teaspoon sugar
¼ teaspoon salt
¼ teaspoon dry mustard
⅛ teaspoon coarsely ground black
     pepper
1 tablespoon cooking oil
2 teaspoons grated gingerroot
2 cloves garlic, minced
2 medium cucumbers, peeled, halved
     lengthwise, seeded, and sliced
     ½ inch thick (2½ cups)
3 green onions, sliced (⅓ cup)
6 cups shredded lettuce
     Lime slices (optional)

Thaw salmon, if frozen. Cut into 1-inch cubes. Discard any skin and bones. Set aside.

For sauce, in a small bowl stir together water, lime peel, lime juice, wine, cornstarch, soy sauce, sugar, salt, dry mustard, and coarsely ground black pepper. Set aside.

Pour cooking oil into a wok or large skillet. (Add more oil as necessary during cooking.) Preheat over medium-high heat. Stir-fry gingerroot and garlic in hot oil for 15 seconds.

Add salmon to the hot wok. Stir-fry for 3 to 6 minutes or till salmon flakes easily, being careful not to break up pieces. Push salmon from the center of the wok.

Stir sauce. Add sauce to the center of the wok. Cook and stir till thickened and bubbly. Add cucumbers and green onions. Gently stir all ingredients together to coat with sauce. Cook and stir for 1 to 2 minutes more or till heated through. Serve immediately on plates lined with shredded lettuce. Garnish with lime slices, if desired. Makes 4 servings.

Nutrition information per serving: 163 calories, 14 g protein, 11 g carbohydrate, 7 g fat (1 g saturated fat), 15 mg cholesterol, 368 mg sodium, 505 mg potassium.

SHARK AND SHRIMP WITH BROCCOLI

Shark is another excellent choice for stir-frying because of its firm texture.

8   ounces fresh or frozen shark, marlin, or swordfish steaks (1 inch thick)
8   ounces fresh or frozen peeled and deveined medium shrimp
2   tablespoons soy sauce
2   tablespoons dry sherry
1   teaspoon grated gingerroot
¾   teaspoon sugar
1   tablespoon cooking oil
1   clove garlic, minced
4   cups broccoli flowerets
1   medium red or green sweet pepper, chopped (¾ cup)
2   cups hot cooked Chinese egg noodles or fine noodles

Thaw shark and shrimp, if frozen. Cut shark into 1-inch cubes. Discard any skin and bones. In a bowl stir together shark, shrimp, soy sauce, sherry, gingerroot, and sugar. Cover and refrigerate for 30 minutes. Drain shark and shrimp, reserving marinade. Set aside.

Pour cooking oil into a wok or large skillet. (Add more oil as necessary during cooking.) Preheat over medium-high heat. Stir-fry garlic in hot oil for 15 seconds. Add broccoli; stir-fry for 3 minutes. Add sweet pepper; stir-fry for 1 minute more or till vegetables are crisp-tender. Remove vegetables from the wok.

Add *half* of the shark and *half* of the shrimp to the hot wok. Stir-fry for 3 to 6 minutes or till shark flakes easily, being careful not to break up pieces. Remove shark and shrimp from the wok. Repeat with remaining shark and shrimp. Return all shark and shrimp to the wok. Push shark and shrimp from the center of the wok.

Stir reserved marinade. Add marinade to the center of the wok. Cook and stir till bubbly. Return cooked vegetables to the wok. Gently stir all ingredients together to coat with marinade. Cook and stir for 1 to 2 minutes more or till heated through. Serve immediately over hot cooked noodles. Makes 4 servings.

Nutrition information per serving: 298 calories, 28 g protein, 28 g carbohydrate, 8 g fat (2 g saturated fat), 136 mg cholesterol, 695 mg sodium, 612 mg potassium.

SHRIMP WITH BASIL AND FRESH TOMATOES

Plump, juicy shrimp and sun-ripened tomatoes get the zesty taste of the Mediterranean from fragrant garlic and basil in this pasta dish.

12	ounces fresh or frozen peeled and deveined medium shrimp
1	tablespoon cooking oil
1	large onion, chopped (1 cup)
2	cloves garlic, minced
2	cups chopped, plum-shaped or common tomatoes
2	tablespoons snipped fresh basil or 1 teaspoon dried basil, crushed
1	tablespoon drained capers (optional)
½	teaspoon salt
⅛	teaspoon pepper
8	ounces spaghetti or other pasta, cooked and drained
¼	cup finely shredded Parmesan cheese
	Fresh basil leaves (optional)

Thaw shrimp, if frozen. Set aside.

Pour cooking oil into a wok or large skillet. (Add more oil as necessary during cooking.) Preheat over medium-high heat. Stir-fry onion and garlic in hot oil for 2 minutes or till onions are crisp-tender. Remove onion mixture from the wok.

Add shrimp to the hot wok. Stir-fry for 2 to 3 minutes or till shrimp turn pink.

Return onion mixture to the wok. Add tomatoes, basil, capers (if desired), salt, and pepper. Stir all ingredients together. Cook and stir for 1 minute more or till heated through. Serve immediately over hot cooked spaghetti or other pasta. Sprinkle with Parmesan cheese. Garnish with fresh basil leaves, if desired. Makes 4 servings.

Nutrition information per serving: 391 calories, 26 g protein, 55 g carbohydrate, 8 g fat (2 g saturated fat), 136 mg cholesterol, 545 mg sodium, 498 mg potassium.

LEMON SHRIMP AND ASPARAGUS

When buying fresh asparagus, look for thin spears that are less than ½-inch thick in diameter. Thick spears may be tough and stringy.

12 ounces fresh or frozen peeled and deveined medium shrimp

⅔ cup water

1 teaspoon finely shredded lemon peel

3 tablespoons lemon juice

2 tablespoons brown sugar

1 tablespoon cornstarch

1 teaspoon instant chicken bouillon granules

1 tablespoon cooking oil

2 teaspoons grated gingerroot

1 clove garlic, minced

1 pound fresh asparagus, woody ends trimmed, and bias-cut into 1-inch pieces (3 cups)

4 green onions, sliced (½ cup)

2 cups hot cooked rice
    Lemon slices (optional)

Thaw shrimp, if frozen. Set aside.

For sauce, in a small bowl stir together water, lemon peel, lemon juice, brown sugar, cornstarch, and bouillon granules. Set aside.

Pour cooking oil into a wok or large skillet. (Add more oil as necessary during cooking.) Preheat over medium-high heat. Stir-fry gingerroot and garlic for 15 seconds. Add asparagus; stir-fry for 3 to 4 minutes or till crisp-tender. Remove asparagus from the wok.

Add shrimp to the hot wok. Stir-fry for 2 to 3 minutes or till shrimp turn pink. Push shrimp from the center of the wok.

Stir sauce. Add sauce to center of wok. Cook and stir till thickened and bubbly. Return cooked asparagus to wok. Add green onions. Stir all ingredients together to coat with sauce. Cook and stir about 1 minute more or till heated through. Serve immediately over hot cooked rice. Garnish with lemon slices, if desired. Makes 4 servings.

Nutrition information per serving: 248 calories, 18 g protein, 34 g carbohydrate, 5 g fat (1 g saturated fat), 131 mg cholesterol, 372 mg sodium, 370 mg potassium.

SHRIMP LO MEIN

For the carrot flowers, use small hors d'oeuvre cutters to cut flower shapes from carrot slices.

1   pound fresh or frozen peeled and
      deveined medium shrimp
⅓   cup water
3   tablespoons soy sauce
1   tablespoon cornstarch
1   tablespoon cooking oil
2   stalks celery, thinly bias-sliced (1 cup)
1   medium onion, chopped (½ cup)
2   cups shredded cabbage
2   cups fresh pea pods, strings removed,
      or one 6-ounce package frozen pea
      pods, thawed
1   medium carrot, shredded (½ cup)
4   ounces dried Chinese egg noodles or
      linguine, cooked and drained
2   green onions, sliced (¼ cup)
      Carrot flowers (optional)

Thaw shrimp, if frozen. Cut shrimp in half lengthwise. Set aside.

For sauce, in a small bowl stir together water, soy sauce, and cornstarch. Set aside.

Pour cooking oil into a wok or 12-inch skillet. (Add more oil as necessary during cooking.) Preheat over medium-high heat. Stir-fry celery and chopped onion in hot oil for 2 minutes. Add cabbage, fresh pea pods (if using), and carrot; stir-fry for 1 to 2 minutes more or till vegetables are crisp-tender. Remove vegetables from the wok.

Add *half* of the shrimp to the hot wok. Stir-fry for 2 to 3 minutes or till shrimp turn pink. Remove shrimp from the wok. Repeat with remaining shrimp. Return all shrimp to the wok. Push shrimp from the center of the wok.

Stir sauce. Add sauce to the center of the wok. Cook and stir till thickened and bubbly. Return cooked vegetables to the wok. Add hot cooked noodles or linguine, green onions, and thawed frozen pea pods (if using). Toss all ingredients together to coat with sauce. Cook and stir for 1 to 2 minutes more or till heated through. Serve immediately. Garnish with carrot flowers, if desired. Makes 4 servings.

Nutrition information per serving: 308 calories, 26 g protein, 38 g carbohydrate, 5 g fat (1 g saturated fat), 174 mg cholesterol, 1,016 mg sodium, 648 mg potassium.

SHRIMP PICCATA

Lemon, garlic, and white wine characterize this exceptionally easy, but oh-so-elegant, entrée. Accompany the meal with crisp-tender stalks of steamed asparagus and garnish with scored lemon slices.

1	pound fresh or frozen peeled and deveined large shrimp
2	tablespoons all-purpose flour
⅓	cup dry white wine
2	tablespoons lemon juice
1	tablespoon capers, drained
¼	teaspoon salt
⅛	teaspoon pepper
1	tablespoon margarine or butter
2	cloves garlic, minced
2	cups hot cooked brown rice and wild rice
	Lemon slices, halved (optional)

Thaw shrimp, if frozen. In a medium bowl toss shrimp with flour till coated. Set aside.

For sauce, in a small bowl stir together wine, lemon juice, capers, salt, and pepper. Set aside.

Place margarine or butter in a wok or large skillet. (Add more margarine as necessary during cooking.) Preheat over medium-high heat till margarine is melted. Stir-fry garlic in margarine for 15 seconds.

Add *half* of the shrimp to the hot wok. Stir-fry for 2 to 3 minutes or till shrimp turn pink. Remove shrimp from the wok. Repeat with remaining shrimp; remove all shrimp from the wok.

Stir sauce. Add sauce to the hot wok. Cook and stir till sauce is bubbly and reduces slightly. Return shrimp to the wok. Cook and stir about 1 minute more or till heated through. Serve immediately over a mixture of brown rice and wild rice. Garnish with lemon slices, if desired. Makes 4 servings.

Nutrition information per serving: 247 calories, 21 g protein, 27 g carbohydrate, 4 g fat (1 g saturated fat), 174 mg cholesterol, 405 mg sodium, 226 mg potassium.

ALMOND SHRIMP IN PLUM SAUCE

Plums, cucumber, and onion make this sweet-and-sour dish especially tasty. Toasted almonds lend additional flavor and a bit of crunch!

12	ounces fresh or frozen peeled and deveined medium shrimp
¼	cup orange juice
¼	cup water
3	tablespoons sugar
3	tablespoons hoisin sauce
2	tablespoons vinegar
4	teaspoons cornstarch
¼	teaspoon pepper
3	tablespoons slivered almonds
1	tablespoon cooking oil
1½	teaspoons grated gingerroot
1	medium onion, chopped (½ cup)
4	medium red plums, pitted and thinly sliced (2 cups)
1	medium cucumber, seeded and chopped (1¼ cup)
2	cups hot cooked rice

Thaw shrimp, if frozen. Set aside.

For sauce, in a small bowl stir together orange juice, water, sugar, hoisin sauce, vinegar, cornstarch, and pepper. Set aside.

Preheat a wok or large skillet over medium-high heat. Add almonds; stir-fry for 2 to 3 minutes or till golden. Remove almonds from the wok. Let wok cool.

Pour cooking oil into the cooled wok. (Add more oil as necessary during cooking.) Preheat over medium-high heat. Stir-fry gingerroot in hot oil for 15 seconds. Add onion; stir-fry for 3 to 4 minutes or till crisp-tender. Add plums and cucumber; stir-fry for 2 minutes more. Remove plum mixture from the wok.

Add shrimp to the hot wok. Stir-fry for 2 to 3 minutes or till shrimp turn pink. Push shrimp from the center of the wok.

Stir sauce. Add sauce to the center of the wok. Cook and stir till thickened and bubbly. Return plum mixture to the wok. Stir all ingredients together to coat with sauce. Cook and stir for 1 to 2 minutes more or till heated through. Serve immediately with hot cooked rice. Sprinkle with toasted almonds. Makes 4 servings.

Nutrition information per serving: 345 calories, 19 g protein, 51 g carbohydrate, 8 g fat (1 g saturated fat), 131 mg cholesterol, 926 mg sodium, 511 mg potassium.

COCONUT SHRIMP WITH GARLIC

This Thai dish is milder than most but contains ingredients typical of the cuisine—coconut milk, cilantro, chilies, garlic, fish sauce, and lemon grass.

1   pound fresh or frozen peeled and
    deveined medium shrimp
¾   cup canned unsweetened coconut
    milk
2   tablespoons fish sauce
½   teaspoon white pepper
1   tablespoon cooking oil
4   cloves garlic, minced
12 ounces fresh asparagus, woody ends
    trimmed, and bias-cut into
    1-inch pieces (2¼ cups)
8   ounces fresh mushrooms, quartered
    (3 cups)
2   cups hot cooked rice
2   tablespoons snipped cilantro or
    parsley
    Cilantro or parsley sprigs (optional)

Thaw shrimp, if frozen. Set aside.

For sauce, in a small bowl stir together coconut milk, fish sauce, and white pepper. Set aside.

Pour cooking oil into a wok or 12-inch skillet. (Add more oil as necessary during cooking.) Preheat over medium-high heat. Stir-fry garlic in hot oil for 15 seconds. Add asparagus; stir-fry for 2 minutes. Add mushrooms; stir-fry for 1 to 2 minutes more or till vegetables are crisp-tender. Remove vegetables from the wok.

Add *half* of the shrimp to the hot wok. Stir-fry for 2 to 3 minutes or till shrimp turn pink. Remove shrimp from the wok. Repeat with remaining shrimp. Return all shrimp to the wok. Push shrimp from center of wok.

Stir sauce. Add sauce to the center of the wok. Cook and stir till bubbly. Return cooked vegetables to the wok. Stir all ingredients together to coat with sauce. Cook and stir 1 minute more or till heated through. Toss together rice and snipped cilantro or parsley. Arrange rice mixture on a serving platter or 4 individual plates. Spoon shrimp mixture over rice mixture. Serve immediately. Garnish with cilantro or parsley sprigs, if desired. Makes 4 servings.

Nutrition information per serving: 375 calories, 25 g protein, 30 g carbohydrate, 17 g fat (10 g saturated fat), 177 mg cholesterol, 487 mg sodium, 697 mg potassium.

SHANGHAI SHRIMP AND SCALLOPS

Crushed red pepper adds a bit of zip to the slightly sweet and pungent flavors of this seafood stir-fry. Add more red pepper if you like it hot, or omit it entirely for a milder taste.

8 ounces fresh or frozen peeled and
   deveined medium shrimp
8 ounces fresh or frozen sea scallops
1 tablespoon soy sauce
1 tablespoon dry sherry
2 teaspoons cornstarch
3 tablespoons soy sauce
2 tablespoons brown sugar
2 tablespoons vinegar
2 tablespoons dry sherry
1½ teaspoons cornstarch
1 to 2 teaspoons toasted sesame oil
¼ teaspoon crushed red pepper
1 tablespoon cooking oil
4 cloves garlic, minced
4 medium carrots, thinly bias-sliced
   (2 cups)
3 green onions, slivered or thinly sliced
2 cups hot cooked rice
   Crushed red pepper (optional)

Thaw shrimp and scallops, if frozen. Cut any large scallops in half. In a medium bowl stir together shrimp, scallops, 1 tablespoon soy sauce, 1 tablespoon sherry, and 2 teaspoons cornstarch. Cover and refrigerate for 1 hour. Drain shrimp and scallops, reserving marinade.

For sauce, in a small bowl stir together 3 tablespoons soy sauce, brown sugar, vinegar, 2 tablespoons sherry, 1½ teaspoons cornstarch, sesame oil, ¼ teaspoon crushed red pepper, and reserved marinade. Set aside.

Pour cooking oil into a wok or large skillet. (Add more cooking oil as necessary during cooking.) Preheat over medium-high heat. Stir-fry garlic in hot oil for 15 seconds. Add carrots; stir-fry for 4 to 5 minutes or till crisp-tender. Remove carrots from the wok.

Add *half* of the shrimp and *half* of the scallops to the hot wok. Stir-fry for 2 to 3 minutes or till shrimp turn pink and scallops turn opaque. Remove shrimp and scallops from the wok. Repeat with remaining shrimp and scallops. Return all shrimp and scallops to the wok. Push shrimp and scallops from the center of the wok.

Stir sauce. Add sauce to the center of the wok. Cook and stir till thickened and bubbly. Return carrots to the wok. Add green onions. Stir all ingredients together to coat with sauce. Cook and stir for 1 to 2 minutes more or till heated through. Serve immediately over hot cooked rice. Sprinkle with additional crushed red pepper, if desired. Makes 4 servings.

Nutrition information per serving: 306 calories, 21 g protein, 40 g carbohydrate, 6 g fat (1 g saturated fat), 104 mg cholesterol, 1,237 mg sodium, 527 mg potassium.

SCALLOPS IN CURRY SAUCE

Because of their larger size, sea scallops work better than bay scallops for stir-frying. Choose scallops that are firm, sweet smelling, and free of excess cloudy liquid.

12   ounces fresh or frozen sea scallops
 1   cup water
 1   tablespoon cornstarch
 2   teaspoons soy sauce
 1   teaspoon sugar
 1   tablespoon cooking oil
 2   teaspoons grated gingerroot
 4   cloves garlic, minced
 3   stalks celery, thinly bias-sliced
        (1½ cups)
 2   medium carrots, thinly bias-sliced
        (1 cup)
 4   ounces fresh mushrooms, quartered
        (1½ cups)
 4   green onions, cut into 1-inch pieces
        (⅔ cup)
 1   teaspoon curry powder
 2   cups hot cooked rice
 ⅓   cup chutney
        Toasted pita wedges (optional)

Thaw scallops, if frozen. Cut any large scallops in half. Set aside.

For sauce, in a small bowl stir together water, cornstarch, soy sauce, and sugar. Set aside.

Pour cooking oil into a wok or large skillet. (Add more oil as necessary during cooking.) Preheat over medium-high heat. Stir-fry gingerroot and garlic in hot oil for 15 seconds. Add celery and carrots; stir-fry for 2 minutes. Add mushrooms and green onions; stir-fry for 1 minute. Sprinkle curry powder over vegetables. Stir-fry for 1 minute more or till vegetables are crisp-tender. Remove vegetables from the wok.

Add scallops to the hot wok. Stir-fry about 2 minutes or till scallops turn opaque. Push scallops from the center of the wok.

Stir sauce. Add sauce to the center of the wok. Cook and stir till thickened and bubbly. Return cooked vegetables to the wok. Gently stir all ingredients together to coat with sauce. Cook and stir for 1 to 2 minutes more or till heated through. Serve immediately with hot cooked rice, chutney, and, if desired, pita wedges. Makes 4 servings.

Nutrition information per serving: 290 calories, 15 g protein, 48 g carbohydrate, 5 g fat (1 g saturated fat), 25 mg cholesterol, 359 mg sodium, 662 mg potassium.

SCALLOPS ALFREDO

For extra flavor in this creamy rich recipe, be sure to use freshly shredded Parmesan cheese.

12 ounces fresh or frozen sea scallops
1⅓ cups half-and-half, light cream,
      or milk
3 tablespoons snipped parsley
1 tablespoon cornstarch
¼ teaspoon pepper
1 tablespoon cooking oil
3 cloves garlic, minced
6 ounces spinach fettuccine or plain
      fettuccine, cooked and drained
1 large tomato, cut into wedges
½ cup finely shredded Parmesan cheese
    Finely shredded Parmesan cheese
      (optional)
    Parsley sprigs (optional)

Thaw scallops, if frozen. Cut any large scallops in half. Set aside.

For sauce, in a small bowl stir together half-and-half, light cream, or milk; parsley; cornstarch; and pepper. Set aside.

Pour cooking oil into a wok or large skillet. (Add more oil as necessary during cooking.) Preheat over medium-high heat. Stir-fry garlic in hot oil for 15 seconds.

Add scallops to the hot wok. Stir-fry about 2 minutes or till scallops turn opaque. Push scallops from the center of the wok.

Stir sauce. Add sauce to center of wok. Cook and stir till thickened and bubbly. Cook and stir 2 minutes more. Add cooked fettuccine, tomato, and ½ cup Parmesan cheese. Stir all ingredients together to coat with sauce. Cook and stir for 1 to 2 minutes more or till heated through. Serve immediately. Sprinkle with additional Parmesan cheese and garnish with parsley sprigs, if desired. Makes 4 servings.

Nutrition information per serving: 416 calories, 25 g protein, 40 g carbohydrate, 18 g fat (6 g saturated fat), 65 mg cholesterol, 341 mg sodium, 496 mg potassium.

SCALLOPS WITH PEA PODS AND CORN

Miniature ears of corn, crisp-tender pea pods, and cherry tomatoes make scallops a tantalizing meal, perfect for both quick family fare and easy entertaining.

12 ounces fresh or frozen sea scallops
⅔ cup water
2 tablespoons dry sherry
1 tablespoon cornstarch
2 teaspoons soy sauce
1 teaspoon grated gingerroot
½ teaspoon instant chicken bouillon granules
1 tablespoon cooking oil
2 cups fresh pea pods, strings removed, or one 6-ounce package frozen pea pods, thawed
½ of an 8-ounce package frozen whole baby sweet corn, thawed, or one 8¾-ounce can whole baby sweet corn, drained
16 cherry tomatoes, cut into quarters
3 green onions, sliced (⅓ cup)
2 cups hot cooked ramen or other fine noodles

Thaw scallops, if frozen. Cut any large scallops in half. Set aside.

For sauce, in a small bowl stir together water, sherry, cornstarch, soy sauce, gingerroot, and bouillon granules. Set aside.

Pour cooking oil into a wok or large skillet. (Add more oil as necessary during cooking.) Preheat over medium-high heat. Stir-fry fresh pea pods (if using) and corn in hot oil for 1 to 2 minutes or till crisp-tender. Remove vegetables from the wok.

Add scallops to the hot wok. Stir-fry about 2 minutes or till scallops turn opaque. Push scallops from the center of the wok.

Stir sauce. Add sauce to the center of the wok. Cook and stir till thickened and bubbly. Return cooked vegetables to the wok. Add thawed frozen pea pods (if using), tomatoes, and green onions. Stir all ingredients together to coat with sauce. Cook and stir 1 to 2 minutes more or till heated through. Serve immediately over hot cooked noodles. Makes 4 servings.

Nutrition information per serving: 247 calories, 17 g protein, 26 g carbohydrate, 9 g fat (1 g saturated fat), 43 mg cholesterol, 833 mg sodium, 657 mg potassium.

SCALLOPS AND ARTICHOKES

Couscous, a tiny pasta, originated in North Africa and has gained popularity in this country. That's because it's so easy on the cook—just add boiling water, let stand 5 minutes, and it's perfect every time.

1 **pound fresh or frozen sea scallops**
¾ **cup water**
1 **tablespoon cornstarch**
½ **teaspoon finely shredded lime peel**
1 **tablespoon lime juice**
1 **teaspoon sugar**
1 **teaspoon instant chicken bouillon granules**
⅛ **teaspoon pepper**
1 **9-ounce package frozen artichoke hearts**
1 **tablespoon cooking oil**
½ **of a medium green sweet pepper, cut into thin strips (½ cup)**
½ **of a medium red sweet pepper, cut into thin strips (½ cup)**
2 **cups hot cooked couscous or rice**
   Finely shredded lime peel (optional)

Thaw scallops, if frozen. Cut any large scallops in half. Set aside.

For sauce, in a small bowl stir together water, cornstarch, ½ teaspoon lime peel, lime juice, sugar, bouillon granules, and pepper. Set aside.

Run cold water over artichoke hearts till partially thawed. Cut any large artichoke hearts in half. Set aside.

Pour cooking oil into a wok or large skillet. (Add more oil as necessary during cooking.) Preheat over medium-high heat. Stir-fry artichoke hearts and green and red sweet peppers in hot oil for 1½ to 3 minutes or till sweet peppers are crisp-tender. Remove vegetables from the wok.

Add *half* of the scallops to the hot wok. Stir-fry about 2 minutes or till scallops turn opaque. Remove scallops from the wok. Repeat with remaining scallops. Return all scallops to the wok. Push scallops from the center of the wok.

Stir sauce. Add sauce to the wok. Cook and stir till thickened and bubbly. Return cooked vegetables to the wok. Stir all ingredients together to coat with sauce. Cook and stir for 1 to 2 minutes more or till heated through. Serve immediately over hot cooked couscous or rice. Sprinkle with additional finely shredded lime peel, if desired. Makes 4 servings.

Nutrition information per serving: 258 calories, 21 g protein, 35 g carbohydrate, 5 g fat (1 g saturated fat), 34 mg cholesterol, 452 mg sodium, 654 mg potassium.

VEGETARIAN FRIED RICE

Transform fried rice from a side dish into a sumptuous meal by adding extra eggs and lots of vegetables.

5   eggs, beaten
1   tablespoon soy sauce
1   tablespoon cooking oil
1   small onion, chopped (⅓ cup)
1   clove garlic, minced
1   tablespoon cooking oil
2   stalks celery, thinly bias-sliced (1 cup)
4   ounces fresh mushrooms, sliced
       (1½ cups)
1   medium green sweet pepper, chopped
       (¾ cup)
4   cups cold cooked rice
1   8-ounce can bamboo shoots, drained
2   medium carrots, shredded (1 cup)
¾   cup frozen peas, thawed
3   tablespoons soy sauce
3   green onions, sliced (⅓ cup)
    Crinkle-cut carrot slices (optional)

In a small bowl combine eggs and 1 tablespoon soy sauce. Set aside.

Pour 1 tablespoon cooking oil into a wok or large skillet. Preheat over medium heat. Stir-fry chopped onion and garlic in hot oil about 2 minutes or till crisp-tender. Add egg mixture and stir gently to scramble. When set, remove egg mixture from the wok. Cut up any large pieces of egg mixture. Let wok cool.

Pour 1 tablespoon cooking oil into the cooled wok or skillet. (Add more oil as necessary during cooking.) Preheat over medium-high heat. Stir-fry celery in hot oil for 1 minute. Add mushrooms and sweet pepper; stir-fry for 1 to 2 minutes more or till vegetables are crisp-tender.

Add cooked rice, bamboo shoots, carrots, and peas. Sprinkle with 3 tablespoons soy sauce. Cook and stir for 4 to 6 minutes or till heated through. Add cooked egg mixture and green onions; cook and stir about 1 minute more or till heated through. Serve immediately. Garnish with carrot slices, if desired. Makes 4 to 5 servings.

Nutrition information per serving: 438 calories, 17 g protein, 61 g carbohydrate, 14 g fat (3 g saturated fat), 266 mg cholesterol, 1,177 mg sodium, 606 mg potassium.

BLACK BEAN CHILI

Black beans, sometimes referred to as turtle beans, provide most of the protein for this chunky dish.

1   tablespoon cooking oil
2   cloves garlic, minced
2   medium green sweet peppers, coarsely chopped (2 cups)
1   large onion, chopped (1 cup)
2   medium zucchini, coarsely chopped (2½ cups)
2   cups fresh or frozen whole kernel corn
1   to 2 teaspoons chili powder
1   16-ounce can tomatoes, cut up
1   15- to 16-ounce can black beans, rinsed and drained
1   8-ounce can tomato sauce
1   fresh, pickled, or canned jalapeño pepper, seeded and chopped
½   teaspoon salt
¼   teaspoon pepper
3   cups hot cooked couscous or rice

Pour cooking oil into a wok or 12-inch skillet. (Add more oil as necessary during cooking.) Preheat over medium-high heat. Stir-fry garlic in hot oil for 15 seconds. Add sweet peppers and onion; stir-fry for 2 minutes. Remove pepper mixture from the wok.

Add zucchini and corn to the hot wok; stir-fry for 2 minutes. Add chili powder; stir-fry for 2 minutes more or till vegetables are crisp-tender.

Return pepper mixture to the wok. Add *undrained* tomatoes, black beans, tomato sauce, jalapeño pepper, salt, and pepper. Cook and stir till bubbly. Cover and cook about 5 minutes more. Serve immediately over hot cooked couscous or rice. Makes 4 servings.

Nutrition information per serving: 416 calories, 19 g protein, 85 g carbohydrate, 5 g fat (1 g saturated fat), 0 mg cholesterol, 1,091 mg sodium, 1,367 mg potassium.

PASTA WITH GARDEN VEGETABLES

Two kinds of Italian cheese, Romano and provolone, combine with corkscrew macaroni and an array of fresh vegetables to create supper for four or side-dish servings for half a dozen.

1 tablespoon cooking oil
1 clove garlic, minced
2 small zucchini, sliced ¼ inch thick (2 cups)
1 small yellow summer squash, sliced ¼ inch thick (1 cup)
5 ounces fresh mushrooms, sliced (2 cups)
3 green onions, sliced (⅓ cup)
1 large tomato, diced (1½ cups)
½ teaspoon dried oregano, crushed
⅛ teaspoon pepper
8 ounces corkscrew macaroni, cooked and drained
¼ cup finely shredded Romano or Parmesan cheese
1 cup shredded provolone or mozzarella cheese (4 ounces)
Freshly ground pepper

Pour cooking oil into a wok or large skillet. (Add more oil as necessary during cooking.) Preheat over medium-high heat. Stir-fry garlic in hot oil for 15 seconds.

Add zucchini and summer squash; stir-fry for 3 minutes. Add mushrooms and green onions; stir-fry about 1 minute more or till vegetables are crisp-tender. Add tomato, oregano, and ⅛ teaspoon pepper; stir-fry for 2 minutes more. Remove from heat.

Add hot cooked corkscrew macaroni and Romano or Parmesan cheese to the vegetable mixture. Toss to combine. Serve immediately. Sprinkle with provolone or mozzarella cheese and freshly ground pepper. Makes 4 servings.

Nutrition information per serving: 412 calories, 19 g protein, 53 g carbohydrate, 14 g fat (7 g saturated fat), 27 mg cholesterol, 340 mg sodium, 520 mg potassium.

VEGETABLES WITH TOFU

Bean curd, called tofu by the Japanese, is a rich source of protein made from soy beans in a process similar to cheese making. It also is low in fat, contains no cholesterol, and is inexpensive.

4   dried shiitake mushrooms
2   ounces bean threads (cellophane noodles)
3   tablespoons water
3   tablespoons soy sauce
2   teaspoons sugar
1   teaspoon toasted sesame oil
1   tablespoon cooking oil
1½   cups small cauliflower flowerets
2   medium carrots, thinly sliced (1 cup)
1   medium onion, cut into thin wedges
4   ounces fresh medium mushrooms, quartered (1½ cups)
1   9-ounce package frozen French-style green beans, thawed
1   8-ounce can bamboo shoots, drained
8   ounces firm tofu (bean curd), well-drained and cut into ½-inch pieces
     Carrot roses (optional)
     Cilantro or parsley sprigs (optional)

In a small bowl cover shiitake mushrooms with warm water. Let soak for 30 minutes. Rinse and squeeze to drain thoroughly. Cut mushroom caps into thin slices. Discard stems. Set aside.

Soak bean threads in enough warm water to cover for 30 minutes. Drain well. Cut into 3-inch lengths. Set aside.

For sauce, in a small bowl stir together, 3 tablespoons water, soy sauce, sugar, and sesame oil. Set aside.

Pour cooking oil into a wok or 12-inch skillet. (Add more cooking oil as necessary during cooking.) Preheat over medium-high heat. Stir-fry cauliflower in hot oil for 2 minutes. Add carrots and onion; stir-fry for 2 minutes. Add fresh mushrooms; stir-fry for 1 minute. Add thawed green beans, bamboo shoots, shiitake mushrooms, and bean threads; stir-fry about 2 minutes more or till vegetables are crisp-tender.

Stir sauce. Add sauce to the hot wok. Add tofu. Gently stir all ingredients together to coat with sauce. Cover and cook for 1 to 2 minutes more or till heated through. Serve immediately. Garnish with carrot roses and cilantro or parsley sprigs, if desired Makes 4 servings.

Nutrition information per serving: 260 calories, 13 g protein, 34 g carbohydrate, 10 g fat (1 g saturated fat), 0 mg cholesterol, 812 mg sodium, 699 mg potassium.

MIXED VEGETABLES WITH GOUDA

Dutch Gouda or it's lower-fat cousin, Edam, is melted with a melange of vegetables for a mild creamy sauce. Try the smoked variety of these cheeses for a stronger, more robust taste.

1 tablespoon cooking oil

4 medium carrots, thinly bias-sliced (2 cups)

1 medium zucchini, thinly bias-sliced (1¼ cups)

8 ounces fresh medium mushrooms, quartered (3 cups)

1 medium green sweet pepper, cut into thin 2-inch strips (1 cup)

3 green onions, sliced (⅓ cup)

1 teaspoon dried savory, crushed

⅛ teaspoon pepper

2 cups shredded Gouda or Edam cheese (8 ounces)

1 tablespoon all-purpose flour

4 English muffins, split and toasted
  Fresh fruit (optional)

Pour oil into a wok or 12-inch skillet. (Add more oil as necessary during cooking.) Preheat over medium-high heat. Stir-fry carrots in hot oil for 2 minutes. Add zucchini; stir-fry for 1 minute. Add mushrooms and sweet pepper; stir-fry for 1 minute.

Add green onions, savory, and pepper; stir-fry about 2 minutes more or till vegetables are crisp-tender. Remove from heat.

Toss Gouda or Edam cheese with flour. Gradually stir cheese mixture into vegetables. Stir till cheese is melted. Spoon immediately over toasted English muffin halves. Serve with fresh fruit, if desired. Makes 4 servings.

Nutrition information per serving: 456 calories, 22 g protein, 47 g carbohydrate, 21 g fat (11 g saturated fat), 64 mg cholesterol, 907 mg sodium, 1,064 mg potassium.

MU SHU VEGETABLE ROLL-UPS

Instead of wrapping up our Mu Shu vegetables in the traditional Peking pancakes, we went Mexican and used ready-made flour tortillas. For easier handling, be sure to warm the tortillas before filling.

2 tablespoons water
2 tablespoons soy sauce
½ teaspoon sugar
½ teaspoon cornstarch
8 to 10 8-inch flour tortillas
1 tablespoon cooking oil
1 teaspoon grated gingerroot
2 cloves garlic, minced
2 medium carrots, cut into julienne
   strips (1 cup)
½ of a small head of cabbage, shredded
   (3 cups)
1 medium zucchini, cut into julienne
   strips (1¼ cups)
8 ounces fresh bean sprouts (2 cups)
4 ounces fresh mushrooms, sliced
   (1½ cups)
½ of a medium jicama, peeled and cut
   into julienne strips (1 cup)
8 ounces firm tofu (bean curd), well
   drained and cut into ¾-inch cubes
8 green onions, sliced (1 cup)
¼ cup hoisin sauce
   Cherry tomato flowers (optional)
   Green onion brushes (optional)

For sauce, in a small bowl stir together water, soy sauce, sugar, and cornstarch. Set aside.

Stack tortillas; wrap in foil. Heat in a 350° oven for 10 minutes or till warm. *Or,* place tortillas, *half* at a time, between layers of microwave-safe paper towels. Micro-cook on 100% power (high) for 1½ to 2 minutes or till warm.

Meanwhile, pour oil into a wok or large skillet. (Add more oil as necessary during cooking.) Preheat over medium-high heat. Stir-fry gingerroot and garlic in hot oil for 15 seconds. Add carrots; stir-fry for 1 minute. Add cabbage and zucchini; stir-fry for 1 minute. Add bean sprouts, mushrooms, and jicama; stir-fry for 1 to 2 minutes more or till vegetables are crisp-tender. Push vegetables from the center of the wok.

Stir sauce. Add sauce to the center of the wok. Cook and stir till thickened and bubbly. Add tofu and green onions. Gently stir all ingredients together to coat with sauce. Cover and cook for 2 minutes more or till heated through.

Spread warm tortillas with hoisin sauce. Spoon vegetable mixture onto each tortilla. Fold over one side of the tortilla to cover some of the filling. Then, fold the two adjacent sides of the tortilla over the filling. Secure with toothpicks, if necessary. Serve immediately. Garnish with tomato flowers and green onion brushes, if desired. Makes 4 to 5 servings.

Nutrition information per serving: 399 calories, 20 g protein, 57 g carbohydrate, 12 g fat (2 g saturated fat), 0 mg cholesterol, 1,811 mg sodium, 277 mg potassium.

MANDARIN TOFU STIR-FRY

Tofu takes on the flavors you mix with it. In this case, a sweet-and-sour sauce does the trick.

½   cup sweet-and-sour sauce
⅛   teaspoon ground red pepper
1   tablespoon cooking oil
6   green onions, bias-sliced into 1-inch
     pieces (1 cup)
½   of a red or green sweet pepper, cut
     into strips (½ cup)
2   cups fresh pea pods, strings removed,
     or one 6-ounce package frozen pea
     pods, thawed
1   pound firm tofu (bean curd), well-
     drained and cut into ¾-inch cubes
1   11-ounce can mandarin orange
     sections, drained, or 3 medium
     oranges, peeled and sectioned
2   cups hot cooked rice
2   tablespoons unsalted dry roasted
     peanuts

For sauce, in a small bowl stir together sweet-and-sour sauce and ground red pepper. Set aside.

Pour cooking oil into a wok or large skillet. (Add more oil as necessary during cooking.) Preheat over medium-high heat. Stir-fry green onions and sweet pepper in hot oil for 1 minute. Add fresh pea pods (if using); stir-fry for 1 to 2 minutes more or till vegetables are crisp-tender. Push vegetables from the center of the wok.

Add sauce to the center of the wok. Cook and stir till sauce is bubbly. Add tofu, orange sections, and thawed frozen pea pods (if using). Gently stir all ingredients together to coat with sauce. Cover and cook for 1 to 2 minutes more or till heated through. Serve immediately with hot cooked rice. Sprinkle with peanuts. Makes 4 servings.

Nutrition information per serving: 360 calories, 15 g protein, 53 g carbohydrate, 12 g fat (2 g saturated fat), 0 mg cholesterol, 117 mg sodium, 386 mg potassium.

SESAME VEGETABLES

Soy sauce, ginger, and garlic are frequently used in concert to flavor many Chinese-style dishes. In this dish, the addition of toasted sesame oil and sesame seeds gives the vegetables an added flavor boost.

2   tablespoons soy sauce
½   teaspoon sugar
½   teaspoon toasted sesame oil
1   tablespoon cooking oil
1   teaspoon grated gingerroot
2   cloves garlic, minced
2   cups broccoli flowerets
12 ounces fresh asparagus, woody ends
      trimmed, and bias-cut into 1-inch
      pieces (2 cups)
2   small yellow summer squash, halved
      lengthwise and sliced ¼ inch thick
      (2 cups)
4   ounces fresh mushrooms, sliced
      (1½ cups)
1   tablespoon sesame seed
2   green onions, sliced (¼ cup)

For sauce, in a small bowl stir together soy sauce, sugar, and sesame oil. Set aside.

Pour cooking oil into a wok or 12-inch skillet. (Add more oil as necessary during cooking.) Preheat over medium-high heat. Stir-fry gingerroot and garlic in hot oil for 15 seconds. Add broccoli and asparagus; stir-fry about 4 minutes or till vegetables are crisp-tender. Remove broccoli mixture from the wok.

Add squash, mushrooms, and sesame seed to the hot wok; stir fry for 2 to 3 minutes or till crisp-tender. Return broccoli mixture to the wok. Add green onions.

Pour sauce over vegetables. Cook and stir for 1 to 2 minutes more or till heated through. Serve immediately. Makes 4 to 6 servings.

Nutrition information per serving: 117 calories, 6 g protein, 14 g carbohydrate, 6 g fat (1 g saturated fat), 0 mg cholesterol, 540 mg sodium, 604 mg potassium.

BASIL BEANS AND TOMATOES

The simple addition of fresh basil lends a fragrant scent and flavor to many of your favorite vegetable dishes. Plant some of this easy-to-grow herb in your garden or grow it in a pot on your kitchen window sill.

1   pound fresh green beans, trimmed, or
       two 9-ounce packages frozen whole
       green beans, thawed
1   tablespoon margarine or butter
1   cup sliced fresh mushrooms
2   tablespoons water
4   teaspoons snipped fresh basil or 1
       teaspoon dried basil, crushed
½   teaspoon sugar
½   teaspoon salt
⅛   teaspoon pepper
1½   cups cherry tomatoes, cut into wedges
       Fresh basil sprigs (optional)
       Finely shredded Parmesan cheese
         (optional)

If using fresh green beans, precook, covered, in a medium saucepan in small amount of boiling water for 10 minutes. Drain; set aside.

Place margarine or butter in a wok or large skillet. (Add more margarine as necessary during cooking.) Preheat over medium-high heat till margarine melts. Stir-fry green beans in margarine for 3 minutes.

Add mushrooms; stir-fry for 1 to 2 minutes more or till vegetables are crisp-tender. Add water, basil, sugar, salt, and pepper. Cover and cook about 3 minutes or till just crisp-tender. Add tomatoes; toss to combine. Serve immediately. Garnish with basil sprigs, if desired. Pass Parmesan cheese, if desired. Makes 4 servings.

Nutrition information per serving: 86 calories, 3 g protein, 14 g carbohydrate, 4 g fat (1 g saturated fat), 0 mg cholesterol, 312 mg sodium, 587 mg potassium.

Carrots with Garlic Glaze

Fresh gingerroot, found in this and many other recipes throughout the book, is frequently used in all of the Asian cuisines. When shopping for gingerroot, look for firm roots with smooth, shiny skin.

1   pound carrots, cut into julienne strips
    (3 cups)
¼   cup water
1   tablespoon soy sauce
1   teaspoon cornstarch
    Dash bottled hot pepper sauce
1   tablespoon cooking oil
1   teaspoon grated gingerroot
3   cloves garlic, minced
2   leeks, sliced ½ inch thick (⅔ cup)
    Fresh basil sprigs (optional)

In a medium saucepan precook carrots, covered, in small amount of boiling water for 2 minutes. Drain. Set aside.

For sauce, in a small bowl stir together water, soy sauce, cornstarch, and hot pepper sauce. Set aside.

Pour cooking oil into a wok or 12-inch skillet. (Add more oil as necessary during cooking.) Preheat over medium-high heat. Stir-fry gingerroot and garlic in hot oil for 15 seconds. Add carrots and leeks; stir-fry for 1 to 2 minutes or till vegetables are crisp-tender. Push vegetables from the center of the wok.

Stir sauce. Add the sauce to the center of the wok. Cook and stir till thickened and bubbly. Stir all ingredients together to coat with the sauce. Serve immediately. Garnish with fresh basil sprigs, if desired. Makes 4 to 6 servings.

Nutrition information per serving: 105 calories, 2 g protein, 17 g carbohydrate, 4 g fat (1 g saturated fat), 0 mg cholesterol, 333 mg sodium, 310 mg potassium.

PEPPERS AND ZUCCHINI

You can buy sweet peppers in a rainbow of bright colors. Green, red, and yellow are the most common, but orange and purple peppers are also available. Mix and match the different colors in recipes like this one.

2 tablespoons water
1 tablespoon hoisin sauce
1 tablespoon soy sauce
1 tablespoon dry sherry
1½ teaspoons cornstarch
1 tablespoon cooking oil
1 teaspoon grated gingerroot
1 clove garlic, minced
2 medium zucchini, bias-sliced ¼ inch thick (2½ cups)
1 medium onion, cut into thin wedges
8 ounces fresh mushrooms, quartered (3 cups)
2 medium red, yellow, and/or green sweet peppers, cut into thin strips (2 cups)

For sauce, in a small bowl stir together water, hoisin sauce, soy sauce, sherry, and cornstarch. Set aside.

Pour cooking oil into a wok or large skillet. (Add more oil as necessary during cooking.) Preheat over medium-high heat. Stir-fry gingerroot and garlic in hot oil for 15 seconds. Add zucchini and onion; stir-fry for 3 to 4 minutes or till zucchini is crisp-tender. Remove zucchini mixture from the wok.

Add mushrooms and sweet pepper strips to the hot wok; stir-fry about 2 minutes or till crisp-tender. Return zucchini mixture to the wok. Push vegetables from the center of the wok.

Stir sauce. Add sauce to the center of the wok. Cook and stir till thickened and bubbly. Stir all ingredients together to coat with sauce. Serve immediately. Makes 6 servings.

Nutrition information per serving: 61 calories, 2 g protein, 8 g carbohydrate, 3 g fat (0 g saturated fat), 0 mg cholesterol, 348 mg sodium, 365 mg potassium.

HOT AND PUNGENT CABBAGE

Unlike the more familiar green cabbage, Chinese cabbage grows in an elongated head and is more like a cross between celery and lettuce. Savoy cabbage forms a round head with deeply veined leaves and a mild flavor. All three work well in this tasty side dish.

2   tablespoons soy sauce
2   tablespoons cider vinegar
4   teaspoons sugar
½   teaspoon pepper
1   tablespoon cooking oil
1   medium red sweet pepper, cut into
      thin strips (1 cup)
1   medium yellow sweet pepper, cut into
      thin strips (1 cup)
1   medium onion, chopped (½ cup)
1   to 2 fresh, pickled, or canned jalapeño
      peppers, seeded and finely chopped
12   ounces shredded Chinese cabbage,
      savoy cabbage, or green cabbage
      (about 4 cups)

For sauce, in a small bowl stir together soy sauce, vinegar, sugar, and pepper. Set aside.

Pour cooking oil into a wok or large skillet. (Add more oil as necessary during cooking.) Preheat over medium-high heat. Stir-fry red and yellow sweet peppers, onion, and jalapeño peppers in hot oil about 1½ minutes or till vegetables are crisp-tender. Remove pepper mixture from the wok.

Add cabbage to the hot wok. Stir-fry about 1 minute (allow 3 minutes if using green cabbage) or till crisp-tender. Return pepper mixture to the wok.

Stir the sauce. Add the sauce to the wok. Cook and stir about 1 minute more or till heated through. Serve immediately with a slotted spoon. Makes 4 to 6 servings.

Nutrition information per serving: 86 calories, 2 g protein, 13 g carbohydrate, 4 g fat (1 g saturated fat), 0 mg cholesterol, 524 mg sodium, 355 mg potassium.

JICAMA AND PEPPER STIR-FRY

Sometimes called a Mexican potato, jicama (HE-kuh-muh) is used in Mexican, Central American, and Asian cooking. Its white flesh has a delicate flavor and crisp texture much like that of a water chestnut. When lightly cooked, as in this recipe, it retains its crunchy texture.

1 tablespoon cooking oil
½ of a medium onion, cut into wedges
1 teaspoon grated gingerroot
1 clove garlic, minced
2 medium green, yellow, and/or red
   sweet peppers, cut into thin strips
   (2 cups)
8 ounces jicama, peeled and cut into
   2x½-inch pieces (about 1⅓ cups)
2 tablespoons soy sauce
1½ teaspoons sugar
1 tablespoon lemon juice
1 teaspoon toasted sesame oil (optional)

Pour cooking oil into a wok or large skillet. (Add more cooking oil as necessary during cooking.) Preheat over medium-high heat. Stir-fry onion, gingerroot, and garlic in hot oil for 15 seconds.

Add sweet peppers and jicama; stir-fry for 2 minutes. Sprinkle with soy sauce and sugar; stir-fry about 1½ minutes more or till peppers are crisp-tender. Sprinkle with lemon juice and, if desired, toasted sesame oil; stir. Serve immediately. Makes 6 servings.

Nutrition information per serving: 65 calories, 1 g protein, 10 g carbohydrate, 2 g fat (0 g saturated fat), 0 mg cholesterol, 345 mg sodium, 132 mg potassium.

HOT-STYLE GARLIC SPINACH

Serve this Vietnamese-style wilted salad with grilled fish or chicken for a delightful summertime meal.

1   tablespoon cooking oil
¼   teaspoon chili oil
4   cloves garlic, minced
1   small red or yellow sweet pepper, cut into thin strips (¾ cup)
1   10-ounce package cleaned fresh spinach, torn (8 cups)
1½   teaspoons fish sauce or soy sauce
⅛   teaspoon pepper

Pour cooking oil and chili oil into a wok or 12-inch skillet. (Add more cooking oil as necessary during cooking.) Preheat over medium-high heat. Stir-fry garlic in hot oil for 15 seconds.

Add sweet pepper; stir-fry for 2 minutes. Add spinach; stir-fry for 2 to 3 minutes or just till spinach is wilted. (Add 1 tablespoon water if spinach mixture is dry.)

Stir in fish sauce or soy sauce and pepper. Serve immediately with a slotted spoon. Makes 3 to 4 servings.

Nutrition information per serving: 91 calories, 5 g protein, 9 g carbohydrate, 6 g fat (1 g saturated fat), 0 mg cholesterol, 212 mg sodium, 894 mg potassium.

APPLE-CARROT STIR-FRY

Enjoy this savory apple dish as an accompaniment to stuffed pork chops or roast chicken.

1   tablespoon cooking oil
2   medium carrots, thinly sliced (1 cup)
1   medium onion, cut into wedges and
       halved crosswise
3   medium cooking apples, peeled,
       cored, and sliced (3 cups)
1   tablespoon sugar
¼   teaspoon salt
2   tablespoons water
    Ground nutmeg (optional)

Pour cooking oil into a wok or large skillet. (Add more oil as necessary during cooking.) Preheat over medium-high heat. Stir-fry carrots in hot oil for 2 minutes. Add onion; stir-fry for 2 to 3 minutes or till crisp-tender. Remove vegetables from the wok.

Add apples to the hot wok; stir-fry for 2 minutes. Sprinkle with sugar and salt. Carefully add water. Cover and cook over medium heat for 3 minutes or till apples are just tender. Return cooked vegetables to the wok. Cook and stir till heated through. Sprinkle with nutmeg, if desired. Serve immediately. Makes 4 servings.

Nutrition information per serving: 126 calories, 1 g protein, 24 g carbohydrate, 4 g fat (1 g saturated fat), 0 mg cholesterol, 145 mg sodium, 255 mg potassium.

BEAN SPROUT STIR-FRY

You'll find this appealing combination of vegetable textures, shapes, and colors to be a good complement for grilled steak and chicken.

1 tablespoon cooking oil
1 small zucchini, bias-sliced ¼ inch thick (1 cup)
1 small onion, cut into thin wedges
1 cup sliced mushrooms
1 small red sweet pepper, cut into thin strips (¾ cup)
8 ounces fresh bean sprouts (2 cups)
1 tablespoon soy sauce
½ teaspoon sugar
⅛ teaspoon pepper

Pour cooking oil into a wok or large skillet. (Add more oil as necessary during cooking.) Preheat over medium-high heat. Stir-fry zucchini and onion in hot oil for 3 to 4 minutes or till crisp-tender. Remove zucchini mixture from the wok.

Add mushrooms and sweet pepper to hot wok. Stir-fry for 1 to 1½ minutes or till crisp-tender. Remove mushroom mixture from wok.

Add bean sprouts, soy sauce, sugar, and pepper to the hot wok. Stir-fry for 1 to 2 minutes or till bean sprouts are crisp-tender. Return the zucchini mixture and the mushroom mixture to the wok. Cook and stir gently till heated through. Serve immediately. Makes 4 servings.

Nutrition information per serving: 64 calories, 2 g protein, 7 g carbohydrate, 4 g fat (1 g saturated fat), 0 mg cholesterol, 265 mg sodium, 257 mg potassium.

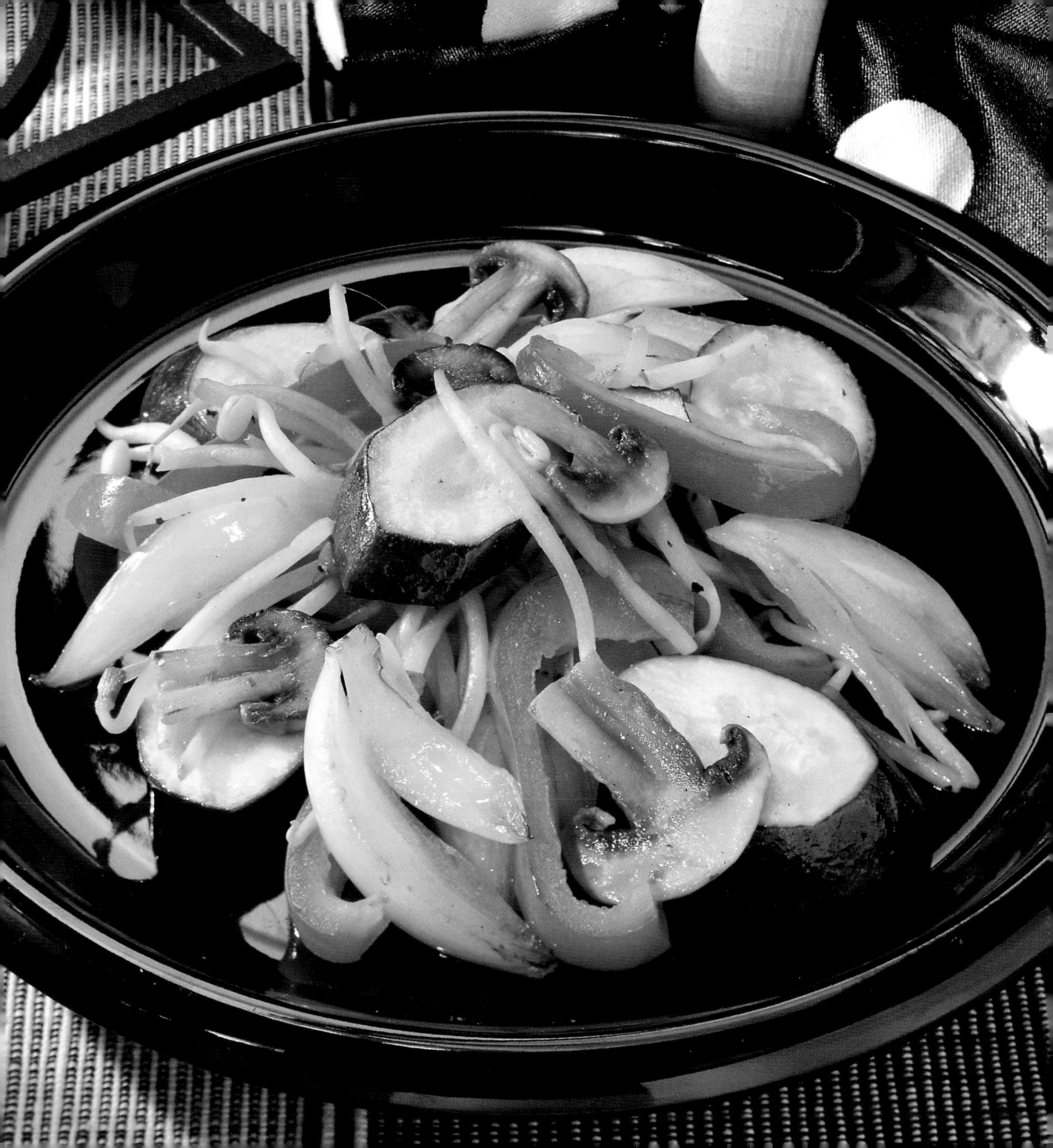

BUTTER-GLAZED SUMMER VEGETABLES

This simple dish enhances the natural goodness of summer vegetables with a generous sprinkling of fresh, fragrant herbs and just a dab of butter.

1 tablespoon cooking oil
2 small zucchini, thinly bias-sliced (2 cups)
2 small yellow summer squash, thinly bias-sliced (2 cups)
2 cups broccoli flowerets
2 teaspoons snipped fresh basil or ¾ teaspoon dried basil, crushed
2 teaspoons snipped fresh oregano or ¾ teaspoon dried oregano, crushed
¼ teaspoon salt
⅛ teaspoon pepper
1 medium tomato, chopped
1 tablespoon butter or margarine

Pour cooking oil into a wok or large skillet. (Add more oil as necessary during cooking.) Preheat over medium-high heat. Stir-fry zucchini and yellow squash in hot oil for 3 to 4 minutes or till crisp-tender. Remove vegetables from the wok.

Add broccoli, basil, oregano, salt, and pepper to the hot wok. Stir-fry for 2 to 3 minutes or till crisp-tender.

Return cooked zucchini and yellow squash to the wok. Add tomato and butter or margarine. Stir-fry just till butter is melted. Serve immediately. Makes 4 to 6 servings.

Nutrition information per serving: 97 calories, 3 g protein, 8 g carbohydrate, 7 g fat (2 g saturated fat), 8 mg cholesterol, 187 mg sodium, 508 mg potassium.

A-B

Almond Shrimp in Plum
  Sauce, 95
Apples
  Apple-Carrot Stir-Fry, 137
  Chicken and Apple Stir-
    Fry, 52
  Chicken Piccadillo, 45
Apricots
  Pork with Apricots and
    Peppers, 38
  Turkey-Apricot Stir-Fry, 65
Artichokes, Scallops and, 106
Asian Vinegar Chicken, 54
Asparagus
  Coconut Shrimp with
    Garlic, 96
  Lemon Shrimp and
    Asparagus, 89
  Sesame Vegetables, 122
Bamboo Shoots
  Curried Chicken Siam, 40
  Swordfish in Chili Sauce, 79
  Szechwan Beef Stir-Fry, 23
  Vegetables with Tofu, 114
  Vegetarian Fried Rice, 108
Basil Beans and Tomatoes, 124
Bean Sprouts
  Bean Sprout Stir-Fry, 138
  Mu Shu Vegetable
    Roll-Ups, 119

*Keep track of your daily
nutrition needs by using the
information we provide at
the end of each recipe.
We've analyzed the nutri-
tional content of each recipe
serving for you. When a
recipe gives an ingredient
substitution, we used the
first choice in the analysis.
If it makes a range of servings (such as 4 to 6), we
used the smallest number.
Ingredients listed as optional weren't included in the
calculations.*

Beans
  Basil Beans and Tomatoes, 124
  Black Bean Chili, 111
  Chicken with Long Beans and
    Walnuts, 63
  Lamb and Bean Ragout, 24
  Vegetables with Tofu, 114
  Warm Turkey Salad, 71
Beef
  Beef and Vegetables in Oyster
    Sauce, 7
  Greek-Style Beef with
    Vegetables, 16
  Orange-Beef Stir-Fry, 21
  Polynesian Stir-Fry, 37
  Southwestern Stir-Fry, 12
  Spicy Thai Ginger Beef, 18
  Sweet-and-Sour Steak, 9
  Szechwan Beef Stir-Fry, 23
  Szechwan Shredded Beef and
    Carrots, 15
  Thai Beef Larnar, 10
Black Bean Chili, 111
Bok Choy
  Asian Vinegar Chicken, 54
  Beef and Vegetables in Oyster
    Sauce, 7
  Szechwan-Style Chicken, 60
Broccoli
  Butter-Glazed Summer
    Vegetables, 141
  Cashew Pork and Broccoli, 31
  Sesame Vegetables, 122
  Shark and Shrimp with
    Broccoli, 84
  Szechwan Beef Stir-Fry, 23
  Szechwan-Style Chicken, 60
  Thai Beef Larnar, 10
  Tuna with Vegetables and
    Linguine, 77
Butter-Glazed Summer
    Vegetables, 141

C-E

Cabbage
  Hot and Pungent
    Cabbage, 130
  Mu Shu Vegetable
    Roll-Ups, 119
  Shrimp Lo Mein, 90
  Stir-Fried Pork and Jicama, 29
Carrots
  Apple-Carrot Stir-Fry, 137
  Carrots with Garlic Glaze, 127
  Country Chicken Stir-Fry, 59
  Greek Lamb Stir-Fry, 27
  Greek-Style Meat with
    Vegetables, 16
  Mu Shu Vegetable
    Roll-Ups, 119
  Scallops in Curry Sauce, 100
  Shanghai Shrimp and
    Scallops, 99
  Shrimp Lo Mein, 90
  Szechwan Beef Stir-Fry, 23
  Szechwan Shredded Beef and
    Carrots, 15
  Vegetables with Tofu, 114
  Vegetarian Fried Rice, 108
Cashew Pork and Broccoli, 31
Chicken
  Asian Vinegar Chicken, 54
  Chicken and Apple Stir-
    Fry, 52
  Chicken Piccadillo, 45
  Chicken Puttanesca, 48
  Chicken with Long Beans and
    Walnuts, 63
  Chicken with Tomato and
    Eggplant, 57
  Country Chicken Stir-Fry, 59
  Curried Chicken Siam, 40
  Fragrant Spiced Chicken, 51
  Honey-Ginger Chicken, 43
  Kung Pao Chicken, 46
  Szechwan-Style Chicken, 60
Coconut Shrimp with Garlic, 96

Corn
  Black Bean Chili, 111
  Scallops with Pea Pods and
    Corn, 105
  Southwestern Stir-Fry, 12
  Szechwan-Style Chicken, 60
Country Chicken Stir-Fry, 59
Creamy Turkey Dijon, 66
Cucumbers
  Almond Shrimp in Plum
    Sauce, 95
  Salmon in Ginger-Lime
    Sauce, 82
  Warm Turkey Salad, 71
Curried Chicken Siam, 40
Eggplant, Chicken with Tomato
    and, 57

F-L

Fish
  Fish Creole, 80
  Salmon in Ginger-Lime
    Sauce, 82
  Shark and Shrimp with
    Broccoli, 84
  Swordfish in Chili Sauce, 79
  Tuna with Vegetables and
    Linguine, 77
Fragrant Spiced Chicken, 51
Greek Lamb Stir-Fry, 27
Greek-Style Beef with Vegetables,
    16
Honey-Ginger Chicken, 43
Hot and Pungent Cabbage, 130
Hot-Style Garlic Spinach, 135
Jicama
  Jicama and Pepper Stir-
    Fry, 132
  Mu Shu Vegetable Roll-Ups,
    119
  Stir-Fried Pork and Jicama, 29
Kung Pao Chicken, 46

Lamb
 Greek Lamb Stir-Fry, 27
 Greek-Style Beef with
  Vegetables, 16
 Lamb and Bean Ragout, 24
 Polynesian Stir-Fry, 37
Lemon Shrimp and Asparagus, 89

M-P
Mandarin Tofu Stir-Fry, 121
Mixed Vegetables with
 Gouda, 116
Mu Shu Vegetable Roll-Ups, 119
Oranges
 Mandarin Tofu Stir-Fry, 121
 Orange-Beef Stir-Fry, 21
 Pineapple-Orange Ginger
  Turkey, 69
Pea Pods
 Beef and Vegetables in Oyster
  Sauce, 7
 Mandarin Tofu Stir-Fry, 121
 Pork and Pear Stir-Fry, 35
 Scallops with Pea Pods and
  Corn, 105
 Shrimp Lo Mein, 90
 Szechwan-Style Chicken, 60
 Turkey-Apricot Stir-Fry, 65
Pear Stir-Fry, Pork and, 35
Peas
 Creamy Turkey Dijon, 66
 Vegetarian Fried Rice, 108
Peppers and Zucchini, 129
Pineapple
 Pineapple-Orange Ginger
  Turkey, 69
 Polynesian Stir-Fry, 37
 Sweet-and-Sour Steak, 9
Polynesian Stir-Fry, 37
Pork
 Cashew Pork and Broccoli, 31
 Polynesian Stir-Fry, 37
 Pork and Pear Stir-Fry, 35
 Pork with Apricots and
  Peppers, 38

Pork (continued)
 Stir-Fried Pork and Jicama, 29
 Szechwan Pork with Peppers,
  32
Potatoes
 Country Chicken Stir-Fry, 59
 Greek-Style Beef with
  Vegetables, 16

S
Salmon in Ginger-Lime Sauce, 82
Scallops
 Scallops Alfredo, 102
 Scallops and Artichokes, 106
 Scallops in Curry Sauce, 100
 Scallops with Pea Pods and
  Corn, 105
 Shanghai Shrimp and
  Scallops, 99
Sesame Vegetables, 122
Shanghai Shrimp and Scallops, 99
Shark and Shrimp with Broccoli,
 84
Shrimp
 Almond Shrimp in Plum
  Sauce, 95
 Coconut Shrimp with Garlic,
  96
 Lemon Shrimp and
  Asparagus, 89
 Shanghai Shrimp and
  Scallops, 99
 Shark and Shrimp with
  Broccoli, 84
 Shrimp Lo Mein, 90
 Shrimp Piccata, 92
 Shrimp with Basil and Fresh
  Tomatoes, 87
Southwestern Stir-Fry, 12
Spicy Thai Ginger Beef, 18
Spinach
 Greek Lamb Stir-Fry, 27
 Hot-Style Garlic Spinach, 135
 Orange-Beef Stir-Fry, 21
Squash
 Butter-Glazed Summer
  Vegetables, 141
 Lamb and Bean Ragout, 24

Squash (continued)
 Pasta with Garden
  Vegetables, 113
 Sesame Vegetables, 122
Stir-Fried Pork and Jicama, 29
Sweet-and-Sour Steak, 9
Swordfish in Chili Sauce, 79
Szechwan Beef Stir-Fry, 23
Szechwan Pork with Peppers, 32
Szechwan Shredded Beef and
 Carrots, 15
Szechwan-Style Chicken, 60

T-Z
Thai Beef Larnar, 10
Tofu
 Mandarin Tofu Stir-Fry, 121
 Mu Shu Vegetable
  Roll-Ups, 119
 Vegetables with Tofu, 114
Tomatoes
 Basil Beans and Tomatoes, 124
 Beef and Vegetables in Oyster
  Sauce, 7
 Black Bean Chili, 111
 Butter-Glazed Summer
  Vegetables, 141
 Chicken Piccadillo, 45
 Chicken Puttanesca, 48
 Chicken with Tomato and
  Eggplant, 57
 Fish Creole, 80
 Greek Lamb Stir-Fry, 27
 Lamb and Bean Ragout, 24
 Pasta with Garden
  Vegetables, 113
 Scallops Alfredo, 102
 Scallops with Pea Pods and
  Corn, 105
 Shrimp with Basil and Fresh
  Tomatoes, 87
 Southwestern Stir-Fry, 12
 Turkey Fajitas, 74
Tuna with Vegetables and
 Linguine, 77
Turkey
 Creamy Turkey Dijon, 66
 Pineapple-Orange Ginger
  Turkey, 69

Turkey (continued)
 Turkey-Apricot Stir-Fry, 65
 Turkey Fajitas, 74
 Turkey Tetrazzini, 73
 Warm Turkey Salad, 71
Vegetables with Tofu, 114
Vegetarian Fried Rice, 108
Warm Turkey Salad, 71
Zucchini
 Bean Sprout Stir-Fry, 138
 Black Bean Chili, 111
 Butter-Glazed Summer
  Vegetables, 141
 Honey-Ginger Chicken, 43
 Mixed Vegetables with
  Gouda, 116
 Mu Shu Vegetable
  Roll-Ups, 119
 Pasta with Garden
  Vegetables, 113
 Peppers and Zucchini, 129
 Polynesian Stir-Fry, 37
 Spicy Thai Ginger Beef, 18

METRIC COOKING HINTS

By making a few conversions, cooks in Australia, Canada, and the United Kingdom can use the recipes in Better Homes and Gardens® *Stir-Fries* with confidence. The charts on this page provide a guide for converting measurements from the U.S. customary system, which is used throughout this book, to the imperial and metric systems. There also is a conversion table for oven temperatures to accommodate the differences in oven calibrations.

Volume and Weight: Americans traditionally use cup measures for liquid and solid ingredients. The chart (top right) shows the approximate imperial and metric equivalents. If you are accustomed to weighing solid ingredients, here are some helpful approximate equivalents.
- 1 cup butter, caster sugar, or rice = 8 ounces = about 250 grams
- 1 cup flour = 4 ounces = about 125 grams
- 1 cup icing sugar = 5 ounces = about 150 grams

   Spoon measures are used for smaller amounts of ingredients although the size of the tablespoon varies slightly among countries. However, for practical purposes and for recipes in this book, a straight substitution is all that's necessary.

   Measurements made using cups or spoons should always be level, unless stated otherwise.

Product Differences: Most of the ingredients called for in the recipes in this book are available in English-speaking countries. However, some are known by different names. Here are some common American ingredients and their possible counterparts:
- Sugar is granulated or caster sugar.
- Powdered sugar is icing sugar.
- All-purpose flour is plain household flour or white flour. When self-rising flour is used in place of all-purpose flour in a recipe that calls for leavening, omit the leavening agent (baking soda or baking powder) and salt.
- Light corn syrup is golden syrup.
- Cornstarch is cornflour.
- Baking soda is bicarbonate of soda.
- Vanilla is vanilla essence.

USEFUL EQUIVALENTS

⅛ teaspoon = 0.5 ml
¼ teaspoon = 1 ml
½ teaspoon = 2 ml
1 teaspoon = 5 ml
¼ cup = 2 fluid ounces = 50 ml
⅓ cup = 3 fluid ounces = 75 ml
½ cup = 4 fluid ounces = 125 ml

⅔ cup = 5 fluid ounces = 150 ml
¾ cup = 6 fluid ounces = 175 ml
1 cup = 8 fluid ounces = 250 ml
2 cups = 1 pint
2 pints = 1 litre
½ inch = 1 centimetre
1 inch = 2 centimetres

BAKING PAN SIZES

American	Metric
8x1½-inch round baking pan	20x4-centimetre sandwich or cake tin
9x1½-inch round baking pan	23x3.5-centimetre sandwich or cake tin
11x7x1½-inch baking pan	28x18x4-centimetre baking pan
13x9x2-inch baking pan	32.5x23x5-centimetre baking pan
2-quart rectangular baking dish	30x19x5-centimetre baking pan
15x10x1-inch baking pan	38x25.5x2.5-centimetre baking pan (Swiss roll tin)
9-inch pie plate	22x4- or 23x4-centimetre pie plate
7- or 8-inch springform pan	18- or 20-centimetre springform or loose-bottom cake tin
9x5x3-inch loaf pan	23x13x6-centimetre or 2-pound narrow loaf pan or paté tin
1½-quart casserole	1.5-litre casserole
2-quart casserole	2-litre casserole

OVEN TEMPERATURE EQUIVALENTS

Fahrenheit Setting	Celsius Setting*	Gas Setting
300°F	150°C	Gas Mark 2
325°F	160°C	Gas Mark 3
350°F	180°C	Gas Mark 4
375°F	190°C	Gas Mark 5
400°F	200°C	Gas Mark 6
425°F	220°C	Gas Mark 7
450°F	230°C	Gas Mark 8
Broil		Grill

Electric and gas ovens may be calibrated using Celsius. However, increase the Celsius setting 10 to 20 degrees when cooking above 160°C with an electric oven. For convection or forced-air ovens (gas or electric), lower the temperature setting 10°C when cooking at all heat levels.